THE

APPLICATION OF THE ROMAN ALPHABET

TO

ALL THE ORIENTAL LANGUAGES

Owing to the antiquity and rarity of this book, certain pages are regrettably absent, and readability is compromised due to the blurring of the original text. If you possess any insights regarding the availability of these missing sections, kindly inform us. Your assistance is crucial in ensuring the completion of this significant work for the benefit of future generations.

THE
APPLICATION OF THE ROMAN ALPHABET
TO
ALL THE ORIENTAL LANGUAGES

CHARLES EDWARD

GYAN

Published by

Gyan Publishing House
5, Ansari Road
Daryaganj, New Delhi-110002
Phone: 011-47034999, 9811692060
E-mail: books@gyanbooks.com

Distribution Network
gyanbooks.com
India, USA, Canada, UK, Australia

ISBN: 978-93-7169-189-5 (PB)

First Published, 1831

2nd Impression 2025

Printed at: Gyan Press, Delhi.

THE APPLICATION OF THE ROMAN ALPHABET
TO ALL THE ORIENTAL LANGUAGES

Author: CHARLES EDWARD

THE APPLICATION OF THE ROMAN ALPHABET TO ALL THE ORIENTAL LANGUAGES;

CONTAINED IN

A SERIES OF PAPERS,

WRITTEN BY

MESSRS. TREVELYAN, J. PRINSEP, AND TYTLER, REV. A. DUFF,

AND MR. H. T. PRINSEP,

AND

PUBLISHED IN VARIOUS CALCUTTA PERIODICALS IN

THE YEAR 1834.

FROM THE SERAMPORE PRESS.

1834.

SELECT PAPERS,

&c.

To the President, Vice Presidents, and Committee of the Calcutta School Book Society.

DEAR GENTLEMEN,

I have the pleasure to submit to your notice an English and Oordoo Dictionary, prepared by Mr. Thompson of Delhi at the request of Mr. Trevelyan, who from acquaintance with his talents considered him well capable of executing such a work. It is designed to assist natives in the Upper Provinces in the acquisition of English, and Europeans in the study of Oordoo. It was expected that the work, if approved, would be printed at the expense of the Society, and as usual 150 copies allowed to the author as a remuneration for his labour; but from a private letter of Mr. Thompson's it appears that 1,000 Rupees is the least he would expect if the Society accept the work, and that he thinks he could realize considerably more than this by printing it himself. Under this view of the case, Mr. Trevelyan and myself think it would be best for the Society to subscribe for 200 copies, and let Mr. T. print for himself. It seems, however, desirable that this subscription for two hundred copies should be made on the express condition that, while the Society consent to Mr. Thompson's receiving the benefit of any edition he may print, he shall allow them to print for themselves if they deem it necessary. Past experience has proved that it is not an eligible plan to employ the resources of the Society in the patronizing of works over which they can have no control, and after the adoption of which into their depository list they cannot pledge themselves for a regular supply. It is better not to adopt, than after having adopted, to be obliged to discard. Should the book be generally approved, and should Mr. T. be willing to submit to these conditions, then I suppose he may be left at liberty to print it where he pleases, stipulating only that it shall be on good English paper, in cloth covers, and not exceeding four Rupees a copy.

I remain,

DEAR GENTLEMEN,

Yours very sincerely,

(Signed) W. YATES, *Secretary.*

Calcutta School Book Society's Depository,
20th November, 1833.

Mr. Thompson's work will doubtless find a ready sale among Europeans, but I trust that none of our colleges has it in contemplation to teach Arabic, Persian, or Hindee words in Roman characters. This would indeed be ultra radicalism, and I cannot therefore vote for any sanction being given by the School Book Society, even in receiving a dedication from the author, unless the words "for the use of European students" be inserted in the title page. Besides, before giving countenance to such an important work as a Dictionary, we should have a report on its execution from some competent person.

(Signed) J. P.

We shall compromise our character very much, particularly with European scholars, in whose eyes the Oriental literature of Calcutta does not, I fear, stand very high at present, if we go back to the old system of printing Oriental books in Roman characters. This is indeed "to mistake the infancy of science for its maturity," and I cannot give my vote for doing so. I am aware that a *School Book Society* is not to publish books of too high an order, but the present appears to me even below our general run of publications, and I am at a loss to see for what class of pupils it can be intended, as it appears ill calculated for any. It is a mere naked vocabulary destitute of every principal of scientific philology in which the words are thrown together in a heap, and full of mistranslations and misapprehensions. A hundred instances might be picked out in a few minutes. In this state it can only serve to puzzle beginners, and will certainly be thrown aside by those who have made the least advance. I think on the whole that the encouragement of such works is a mere waste of funds and therefore vote against it.

(Signed) J. TYTLER.

I owe an apology to the Committee for having suffered a proposition with which my name was connected to be submitted for their decision unaccompanied by any explanation on my part, for I am convinced that if this precaution had been taken, the objections which have been brought forward to Mr. Thompson's work would have been obviated, and the scope and motives of it would have appeared to the members of the Committee in a clearer point of view than has actually been the case. It will now be my endeavour to supply the deficiency as far as it can be done at this late period of the discussion, and I am encouraged to adopt this course by observing that several gentlemen for whose opinions I entertain a high respect, are inclined to view the proposition with favour, while our highly honoured President has suspended the expression of his opinion until the question shall have received more complete elucidation. I shall now proceed to consider each of the objections in the order in which they have been brought forward.

Mr. Prinsep "trusts that none of our colleges has in contem-"plation to teach Arabic, Persian, and Hindee words in Roman "characters. This," he observes, "would indeed be ultra radi-"calism." This is the sole objection assigned by this gentleman to the plan, that it would be "ultra radicalism." Let us consider therefore what ultra radicalism is. It means an *entire* change. Now change is a relative term which may be either good or bad according to the circumstances of each particular case. If the change is good, it is of course desirable that it should be radical; and if it is bad, it were better that it did not take place at all.

This is not the first ultra radicalism in the department of education which has emanated from Delhi.

At Calcutta scarcely any encouragement is offered to the Mahomedans to study English, while they are bribed at an expence of more than 30 Rupees a month for every student to cultivate Arabic;* the consequence of which is that there is scarcely a single Mahomedan to be found at Calcutta who has received a tolerable education. At Delhi equal encouragement is held out to Mahomedans and Hindoos to prosecute the study of English literature and science, and the youth of both denominations are pursuing it there in nearly equal numbers and with equal success. This is an ultra radicalism.

At Calcutta the division of society into castes is carefully cherished and perpetuated by maintaining separate institutions for Christians, Mahomedans, and Hindoos. At Delhi the youth of every religion and caste pursue their studies together in the same institution. This is another ultra radicalism, and so little was it

---

* The following description of this Monkish institution is taken from a note of the Secretary to the Committee of Public Instruction :

"I deem it my duty to notice that the Madrissa has only 74 students, all of whom it supports by pecuniary allowances and that (without taking into consideration the heavy items of printing) the board and tuition of each student costs 320 Rupees per annum, a rate greatly exceeding the expenditure on the pupils of any other institution. It is possible the excess may be counterbalanced by great public advantages."

anticipated by Mr. Wilson that at the first formation of the Delhi College, among other branches of study proposed by him for the new institution, one was the "scheme of castes" in all its complicated ramifications. Happily this kind of propagandism did not take there. Benares has always been more under the influence of Calcutta, and the institutions at that place present an exact counterpart to those at the capital.

I have now submitted to the Committee two instances of ultra radicalisms, and I fearlessly allege that they are both good and contain in themselves the seeds of great prospective improvement. A third has now been produced emanating from the same place, and before Mr. Prinsep can justly call upon the Committee to condemn it, he is bound to shew that it is of a bad and not of a good description. This he has omitted to do, and as yet he has not favoured us with a single reason against the more general introduction of the Roman letters to which he so strongly objects. The subject, however, is of so much importance that I cannot suffer it to be thus cursorily passed over, and I will proceed to answer, as briefly as possible, all the difficulties with which the change can be supposed to be attended.

Perhaps it may be thought that the Roman letters are so strange and foreign to the people of this country, that the extensive use of them in writing the Indian languages cannot reasonably be anticipated. To this I would reply that these letters, which were at first used only for the Latin tongue within the limits of the little territory of Latium, have gradually been adopted to express all the languages of Europe, America, Australia, and part of Africa and Asia. The Greek, the German, and the Russian characters are the sole exceptions to the general uniformity in the mode of writing in Europe, and at last two of these are rapidly falling into disuse. The old German text is now almost entirely abandoned, and few new books are published in Germany except in the Roman character. In Greece the revival of letters has been marked by the simultaneous adoption of the universal written character of the civilized world, and Romaic, or modern Greek, School

Books, Testaments, and, I believe, newspapers also, expressed in Roman letters, are daily becoming multiplied. Both in North and South America, whether the language be English, French, Spanish or Portuguese, the Roman characters prevail, without any exception, and the same in the Australian continent which is in progress of being peopled as yet by Englishmen only. The letters which have been adopted to express the languages of the south sea islanders are also the Roman, with only such modifications as are necessary to denote the sounds peculiar to their tongues, and numerous printing presses are at this moment employed in spreading these universal harbingers of civilization throughout the great Southern Archipelago. The same plan has been pursued in Java, the Celebes, and wherever else the Dutch have had authority, and, as a specimen, I have the honour to submit to the Committee a Testament in the Malay language and Roman character.

The Roman letters have actually been adopted to express the popular languages of India. The plan was introduced by Sir William Jones and zealously followed up by Mr. Gilchrist, and had the latter gentleman been supported by a Society like ours, the system would no doubt by this time have been fully established. Unfortunately, however, for the cause of popular education, the Oriental rage was at the period when Gilchrist laboured, at its height, and he was overborne by a host of learned orientalists, who, in making knowledge simple, foresaw the ruin of their craft. Every body must be aware that when the popular languages of the East are once disencumbered of their Persian or Sanscrit dress, the gentlemen who are the depasitories of Asiatic lore will no longer be looked up to with the same degree of wonder and admiration as they are at present, and they will greatly sink in the estimation of their learned brethren in the West.

The Roman system of letters has now been adopted in India for the third time under happier auspices. The exclusive taste for Oriental studies never extended in its full force to the extremities of the empire. The focus of this influence was at Calcutta, where its intensity was concentrated by a profusion of honours and rewards in the shape of professorships both for Natives and Europeans, secretaryships to Oriental Colleges, moonsheeships, Arabic translationships at the rate of 750 Rupees per 50 pages, studentships in the Arabic College at an expence to the state of more than 30 Rupees a month, &c. &c. There was nothing of this kind in the Upper Provinces. Occasionally, indeed, a stray orientalist made his appearance there, but unfortunately for the profession, his qualifications in other respects did not always sufficiently correspond with his attainments in the science of words to gain many admirers for the system. In the Upper Provinces, therefore, there were no predilections to stand in the way of the new letters, and there was no danger of their being strangled as soon as they were born, as they had formerly been at Calcutta.

Another circumstance which augurs very favourably for the success which is likely to attend the reproduction of the old system, is, that the measure has not been adopted until the necessity of it became self-evident. Great numbers of the youth of Delhi, who are brought up at the English College, have no acquaintance whatever either with the Nagree or Persian character. They know English as their language of education, and Hindoostanee as their vernacular tongue, but the only character with which they are acquainted is the Roman, and this they employ to write both languages. For their use, therefore, (and they are a very intelligent and annually increasing class) an English and Hindoostanee Dictionary was indispensable. Under these circumstances Mr. Thompson undertook the compilation of a small vocabulary which met with such eminent success that he was encouraged to apply himself to the task of preparing the larger work to which the patronage of the Committee is now solicited. The vocabulary is circulated herewith, and it is deserving of attention as the first fruits of a system of letters, which will eventually become universal throughout the East and will contribute in a higher degree to hasten the period when India will possess a national literature of her own equal to any other in the world.

The plan which the Committee is requested to support is, therefore, any thing but an uncertain experiment suggested by the expectation of probable advantage. It is a measure called for by urgent necessity and proved to be advantageous by the result of a trial which has been already made. If there was any thing of speculation in the matter, it was in the original essay made by Mr. Thompson and not in the measure now adopted to follow up a plan, the soundness of which has been fully established.

I beg leave to call the attention of the Committee to the commentary furnished by the facts which have been stated upon the cry now raised of ultra radicalism. The first great change was effected when the Roman letters surpassed the ancient limits of the territory of Rome, and, since that time, by a succession of ultra radicalisms, they have been adopted by one nation after another, until at last they bid fair to become the universal written character of the whole world. Every one of these changes was, no doubt, condemned by the lovers of ancient lore of the day, and, if their advice had been attended to, every nation would to this day have had its own separate character, as well as language, and one more barrier would have been added to those which already stand in the way of the general fraternization of the human race and the general enlightenment of the human mind. In England the Roman letters did not acquire their present well established ascendancy until after several struggles, and the lovers of the Saxon, Norman, Old English, court hand, &c. no doubt, each in their day, strenuously maintained that their own way of writing English was the only one in which the force and beauties of the language could be properly expressed. The ultra radicalism has actually been perpetrated in this country. The Roman letters have taken their place in Indian literature, and notwithstanding the opposition which may be raised by learned orientalists, I am convinced that they will continue to advance by a slow, but sure, progress, until that day shall have arrived when the curse of Babel shall have been removed and all mankind shall have become united in the enjoyment of a common language and a common mode of expressing it.

The Roman is not the first foreign character which has been

adopted to express the popular language of India. The Persian and Arabic characters are equally foreign, and they are not nearly so distinct or so easy to be used in printing as the Roman. The Nagree character also, although quite foreign to the languages of Persia and Arabia, is used to express words of pure Arabic and Persian origin.

The Roman letters are capable of being adapted to the popular languages of India in a much more complete manner than they have been to that of England. Nothing can be more preposterous than our English system of *writing*, for it is not deserving of the name of Orthography. For instance, *hare, hair, heir, were, pear,* are all written differently, although the vowels have precisely the same sound; but in adapting the Roman letters to the popular languages of India, whether Sir Wm. Jones's, Mr. Gilchrist's, or Mr. Thompson's scheme ultimately come into general use, an exact correspondence between the writing and the pronunciation will be preserved.

In the different schemes of letters which have been devised, the varying sounds of the Indian consonants which are not represented by a corresponding letter in the Roman alphabet, have been distinguished by some peculiar mark or by some modification of the kindred letter. I know that the lovers of Arabic and Sanscrit will reply to this, that if any modifications of the Roman alphabet are admitted for the purpose of denoting sounds peculiar to the Indian languages, the system of letters which it is proposed to bring into more extended use, will then be neither one thing nor the other, neither Roman nor Indian. I rejoin by asking whether the Persian character, as used in writing Hindoostanee, is more pure? It is far from being so. In order to adapt the Persian characters to the language of Hindoostan it was necessary to invent signs to distinguish the different variations of sound in the Sanscrit consonants, and the letters peculiar to the Arabic (ain, ghain, toe, zoe,) were introduced without any alteration in the forms in which they are used in writing the original language. The Persian alphabet, therefore, as used in writing the Hindoostanee language, is as great

B

a mongrel as ever the Roman letters can be when they are applied to the same purpose, being made up, partly of pure Persian characters, partly of letters introduced from the Arabic, and partly of certain modified forms of Persian letters which have been invented by the Fort William philologists to represent those sounds of the Sanscrit letters which are not to be found in Persian. This adaptation was not completed until of late years, when the subject was taken up by the learned orientalists of the College of Fort William. They might just as well have modified the Roman as the Persian characters to express the language of this country. They are both equally foreign and equally applicable to it with some slight alterations.

We are not such pedants as to desire to sacrifice both sense and usefulness in the attempt to attain an ideal uniformity. The basis only of the Indo-Roman character is Roman, as the basis of the Indo-Persian character is Persian, and where additions or modifications are required, they have been made. So far as the languages agree, the pure Roman character is used for both, and so far as they differ, a modification of it has been devised suited to meet the exigency of the case. The particulars in which the languages coincide are made evident to the student from the similarity of character, and the points in which they differ are rendered plain to him by the peculiar marks. This, it must be admitted, is a great assistance both to the Englishman learning the Indian, and to the Indian learning the English, language, and besides this, by clearly pointing out the discrepancies between the tongues, a tendency has been created to produce a more exact correspondence between them.

If it were to be asked what advantages are to be expected from adopting the Roman letters as the medium for expressing the Indian languages, I would answer as follows:—

First. The Roman character, whether it be written or printed, is more distinct than any other which can be adopted for expressing the languages of India, whether they be derived from the Sanscrit, Arabic, Persian or English source, or whether they be mixed and compounded of the whole or any number of these tongues. The superiority of the Roman letters may be inferred from the circumstance of their having gradually been adopted, in spite of every opposition, to express the languages of so many different nations in different parts of the world, and notwithstanding the continuance of the same opposition, they are still spreading to a degree far exceeding any other character. One main cause of the superior distinctness of the Roman character is that the vowels are expressed, instead of being either entirely omitted, or distinguished by diacritical points, which are continually liable to be misplaced and left out, and even when every precaution is taken, it is more difficult to read Hebrew, Arabic, or Persian, in which the vowels are represented by minute points, placed above or below the line, than any language printed in Roman characters in which they are denoted by a separate letter standing in its place in the line. Another reason is the extreme neatness of the printed Roman character. The art of printing has been carried to a far higher degree of perfection in these letters than in any others. As they are the universal character of the civilized world, they have been more extensively used in printing than any other, and, from the first invention of the art to the present day, they have been gradually elaborated and improved in the manner which has been found by experience best adapted to meet the difficulties which from time to time have suggested themselves. They have the result of nearly three hundred years experience in their favour, and I put it to the Committee whether it be most desirable to adopt the Roman character, thus perfected and improved, or to go on with the tedious process of elaborating Nagree and Persian by a succession of changes which must be carried through a long series of years before we can hope to arrive at the same degree of perfection.

Secondly. Printing can be carried on in Roman characters much cheaper and more expeditiously than it can either in Persian or in Nagree. For instance, Mr. Pearce informs me that it would cost one-third more and take up double the time to print Mr. Thompson's manuscript in Roman and Nagree or Persian characters united, as it would to print it in Roman characters alone, and after all, it would not be so perfect, if Persian characters formed part of the design, on account of the liability of the numerous vowel and other points used in writing that language to break, to be misplaced, to be omitted, or not to be correctly ascertained; their application varying according to the authority of different Dictionaries. In laying the foundation of a national literature it is of great importance to select a character which will cause as small an expenditure as possible of the time and money of the nation. It is not easy to imagine how much of these important elements of human affairs might be saved in the course of one hundred years by having all our books printed in Roman characters only, which cost one-third less, instead of Persian or Nagree which cost one-third more. To make knowledge cheap and bring books down to the level of the means even of the poorest class of people, it must be admitted, is an object of some importance.

Thirdly. A still greater advantage which will be gained by the plan will be, that the adoption of the Roman characters in India will lead to the gradual disuse of the Nagree and Persian and Arabic ones, and we shall thus have three characters less than we had before. Need I point out the advantages of such a consummation? Next to the multiplicity of languages, the intellect of India is oppressed by the multiplicity of letters, and it is shocking to think how much human time, which might be directed to the best purposes, is wasted in gaining a knowledge of the many barbarous characters with which the country abounds. The student of Hindoostanee now has to learn both the Nagree and Persian characters, and, if he would commence the study of English, he must learn the Roman also; but, under the new plan, the Roman characters will do for all. The infancy of every nation in the pursuit of knowledge is always marked by a diversity of languages and letters, and, as it improves in civilization, they gradually become assimilated and ultimately merge in one common character and tongue. The natural and just tendency of every thing is to simplicity.

Fourthly. It is generally admitted that our endeavours should be mainly directed to the gradual formation of a national literature embodying in itself the selected knowledge of the whole civilized world, and it forms a strong recommendation of the plan now under consideration that it will greatly tend to facilitate the accomplishment of this highly important object. When the languages of England and of India shall become expressed in a character common to both, the obstacles which stand in the way of their assimilation will be materially diminished. The path from one language to the other will be in a manner smoothed to every student, as he will have the words only to learn and not the symbols whereby they are expressed. The person who knows English will be more easily induced to cultivate a tongue embodied in a character with which he is already acquainted, and into which he can introduce pure English words without any glaring impropriety; thereby gratifying his literary taste at the same time that he will be able to convey his meaning with greater readiness and precision in terms taken from the more scientific and cultivated language; while, on the other hand, the Hindoostanee scholar will, for the same reason, enter with greater ease upon the study of English, and draw from it, in like manner, stores of expressive words for the improvement of his Native dialect. In either case, whether the English scholar descend to Hindoostanee, or the Hindoostanee scholar ascend to English, the transition will be made much easier to them both, by the use of a common character and the certain result of this intimate connection between the two languages will be that the national literature will be enriched by plentiful supplies of words and ideas derived from the English source. The words of the English language are so generally indeclinable that their introduction into the Indian dialects may be accomplished with peculiar ease. How desirable would it be to engraft upon the popular languages of the East such words as *virtue*, *honour*, *gratitude*, *patriotism*, *public spirit*, and some others for which it is at present difficult to find any synonym in them!

Lastly. By means of the assimilation proposed, the mutual

good understanding between the two races will be greatly promoted. When their languages shall be expressed in a character common to both, the English will learn more Indian, and the Indians will learn more English. If Latin were to be written in Hebrew, and French in Greek, characters, is it likely that we English should know so much about those languages as we do?

Mr. Prinsep observes, "Mr. Thompson's work will doubtless find a ready sale among Europeans. I cannot vote for any sanction being given by the Society even in receiving a dedication from the author, unless the words *for the use of European students* be inscribed on the title page;" from which we must infer, that, in Mr. Prinsep's opinion, the circumstance that it will also be of use to European students constitutes a ground of objection to the book. For my part, I entertain exactly the contrary opinion, and, that it will be equally useful to all classes, appears to me to be a clear indication that the work is founded on sound principles. If, through the medium of our Society, books can be provided which shall not only facilitate the acquisition of the English language by the natives of India, but shall also assist the natives of England in acquiring a knowledge of the Indian languages, surely no wiser or nobler application could be made of our patronage. This appears to me to be the exact point of union towards which we should direct all our efforts as far as mere language is concerned.

It is asked what class of people will make use of such a Dictionary as Mr. Thompson's. I reply briefly,

First. Those native students of the English language, who, like the Delhi youths, are not acquainted with any character except the Roman.

Secondly. Every native who is engaged in studying the English language. In order to acquire even the slightest knowledge of English, every student must learn the Roman character, and it is obvious that the same degree of acquaintance with it, which enables him to read English imperfectly, would enable him to read his own language fluently. It will be a good way for children to begin to learn the Roman character by reading their own language in it, since a familiarity with any written character is more easily acquired through the medium of one's own than through that of a foreign language. If we wished to teach an English boy the Roman character, we should first set him to read English, and not Latin.

Thirdly. Every person, whether Indian or European, who is already acquainted with English and wishes to obtain an acquaintance with Hindoostanee.

In short, every Englishman who wishes to learn Hindoostanee, and every Indian who wishes to learn English, will take the first four Rupees he has to spare to Mr. Thompson's stall.

In his love for oriental hieroglyphics, Mr. Prinsep has overlooked the fact that to use *any* Hindoostanee and English Dictionary *a native must understand the Roman letters,* unless indeed that gentleman, in his ultra toryism, would express our English words in Sanscrit, Arabic, or Persian characters. The Roman letters must be used and understood, *at any rate,* and why, therefore, should we increase the price of our Dictionary and puzzle the brains of our readers by the addition of barbarous Persian?

Before I conclude this part of the subject, I may as well observe, that it is not expected that the Roman letters can be generally introduced at once. Their complete establishment throughout India, to the exclusion of every other character, must be a work perhaps of several generations. The principle I advocate is the one which is understood to form the leading maxim of our Society, viz. that we should prepare books of a kind suited for every class of readers, and leave it to the popular taste to determine which shall be ultimately adopted and which rejected. I have shewn that there are at present large classes of people to whom an Hindoostanee Dictionary, printed in the Roman character, would be highly acceptable, and, having done so, I conceive that I have made out a sufficient claim for the patronage of the Committee. If the demand for books printed in the Roman character spreads, so much the better, and if not, we shall only have done our duty in supplying an actual call for the means of instruction. Although, therefore, the change of which I am the humble advocate, may some day become radical, in the meantime it will only be gradual.

I shall now proceed to answer the objections brought forward by Mr. Tytler. The learned gentleman is of opinion that we "shall compromise our character, particularly with European scholars, in whose eyes the Oriental Literature of Calcutta does not stand very high at present, if we go back to the old system of printing Oriental books in Roman characters."

To this I reply that our Committee was not established for the purpose of raising the reputation of Calcutta as a seat of Oriental Literature, but for the purpose of providing the means of cheap and easy instruction for the people of the Bengal Presidency. These two objects have heretofore been too much confounded, or to speak more correctly, the latter, which is by far the most important, involving the intellectual and moral welfare of about sixty millions of people, has in a lamentable degree been sacrificed to the former. So long as we remained engrossed in the pursuit of the higher branches of Oriental lore, the education of the people was almost entirely lost sight of by us. The rage for orientalism commenced in the time of Marquis Wellesley. The object which that nobleman had in view was to educate Europeans in the languages of the East. Our object is to educate Asiatics in the sciences of the West. The means adopted by Marquis Wellesley, therefore, whether they were well adapted or not for the ends which he had in view, are totally unsuited to forward the design of our society.

If Lord Wellesley's oriental system had been confined within its proper limits, although it might not have done any good, yet it would not have done much harm ; but, instead of this, it soon exceeded all due bounds and deluged the country with such an inundation of Sanscrit and Arabic, as had not been seen since the time of King Bhoj or Muhmood of Ghuznee. Instead of a revival of sound learning, it was only a revival of antiquated errors, and our orientalists fondly imagined that, while they were propagating the long exploded absurdities of Avicenna or the profligacies of the

Sanscrit dramas, they were promoting the cause of public instruction.

This era of the history of India affords a curious instance of the natural tendency of the human mind to attach an undue degree of importance to those particular pursuits with which it happens to be conversant. The study of Sanscrit and Arabic is unobjectionable as a curious branch of enquiry, to be pursued by men of leisure and literary curiosity who happen to have a turn for the study of different languages, but it is absurd to suppose that the spread of true knowledge and the elevation of the morals of a nation can be promoted by such means.

For about thirty years, all the influence of the state was employed in directing the talent of the country towards the exclusive cultivation of the three dead languages, Sanscrit, Arabic and Persian,* and a high standard of acquirement in any one of them formed a certain avenue to civil employ. There was also another, and a still more powerful, motive to encourage the taste for orientalism, particularly among the English portion of the community. This

---

* The languages of Arabia and Persia, as known in India, are dead languages. If we except a few Arab and Persian merchants, they are the living, spoken languages of no one class of people, and when the natives of the country wish to cultivate them, they are under the necessity of commencing the study of them from the beginning as they would of any other disused tongue. There was a time, no doubt, when they were the living languages of large classes of people in India. But that period has long since passed by, and English has taken the place which they once occupied. The spoken languages of India are the Hindoostanee, Bengalee, &c. which are the languages of the many, and English, which is the language of the few, but although it be the language of the few, English possesses an importance far out of proportion to the numerical amount of the people by whom it is spoken, arising, as well from the superior influence inseparable from our situation in India, as from the superior stores of learning which our language contains. The English language is the source from which we must draw for the improvement of Native literature, and we might as well separate the stream from the fountain or the bread from the leaven which leavens it, as the vernacular dialects from the English language. The two will go on together through successive generations till they meet in a common language, equal for variety and power of expression and for the amount of knowledge which it contains, to any of which the world can boast.

is the one alluded to by Mr. Tytler. By means of the three dead languages, an *European* reputation was to be acquired. Here was a meed worthy of the most aspiring ambition! By the successful study of Sanscrit, Arabic and Persian, a person not only becomes well known in England, but his name is familiarized to the "European scholars" of France and Germany and almost every other European country, for there is none which does not boast of some orientalists.

This would be very well in an Antiquarian Society of European gentlemen, but it will not suffice for our Society which has in view the improvement of an intellectually ignorant and morally degraded people. Let Mr. Tytler continue to pursue his Arabic studies, in the prosecution of which I wish him every success; but let us not suffer ourselves to be persuaded by him that we are instructing the Indians, while we are only gratifying the peculiar literary taste, and I fear, too generally, the vanity of a few European scholars who happen to have turned their attention to the Sanscrit and Arabic languages. Our business is not with Europe, but with India; and our object is to instruct the people of India by the united means of English and of the popular languages, and not to gain a reputation in Europe by a patronage of the learned few who have leisure and inclination to devote themselves to the study of Sanscrit and Arabic. The objection that we shall fail to acquire for ourselves an European reputation and that the bounds of the continent of India will also form the limits of our fame, can therefore have no influence with us. We never meant to aspire to the honour of knighthood, nor did the prospect of filling the oriental chairs in the universities of England ever enter into our imaginations, and when we travel abroad, we shall not feel mortified if we pass unrecognized by the literati of Paris, Bonne and Vienna, never having expected any attention from them. These honours are the rewards of encouraging Sanscrit and Arabic lore. But we shall enjoy the humble satisfaction of having done good in our day and generation, and I am sure that there are some gentlemen on our Committee whose souls are susceptible of being influenced by such a motive. We desire not to claim fraternity with Messrs. Bopp and Schlegel, but we recognize the duty of providing for the mental cultivation and moral improvement of millions of our fellow-subjects, and to this cause we are ready to devote time, and talents, and property, and all we possess that can be spared from other claims.

It may be thought that I have exaggerated the extent to which the instruction of the many has been sacrificed to the literary taste of the few. I beg leave to assure the Committee that such is far from being the case. A statement is annexed of the entire sum which has been expended by the General Committee of Public Instruction from the date of its institution up to the 30th April 1832, in the printing of Oriental works, or in assisting the authors to print them, by taking a certain number of copies off their hands. From an examination of this document it will be seen, that the patronage of the General Committee has been bestowed in the following proportions up to the above-mentioned date :

Sanscrit................	13,000	volumes.
Arabic..................	5,600	ditto.
Persian.................	2,500	ditto.
Hindee..................	2,000	ditto.

Not a single Bengalee or Oordoo book has been printed by the General Committee, nor has one translation been made through their medium into the popular languages. It is true that four Hindee works have been published by them (Subha Bilas, Rajniti, Chutraprakasa, and Dayabhaga,) but none of these convey any European information. Not one of them is a translation of any European book, but they are either reprints of original Hindee books or of old Hindee translations from Sanscrit books ; and they are all classical works, formed on an exclusively Sanscrit model, without a knowledge of which language they are almost unintelligible, and are therefore quite unfit to be used as a medium of popular instruction.

Will it now be said that I have exaggerated? These books were printed at the expense of a fund consecrated by the Parliament of Great Britain to the cause of *popular education*, and they form the result of twelve years labours of the Committee of Public Instruction in that highly important branch of their duty, which consists in the provision of Oriental books for the instruction of the public. Some of these books are of such a nature that the members of the General Committee would at once repudiate the idea of their being intended for the instruction of youth or even of their being at all put into their hands. The Sanscrit drama called the Mricchakata, or Toy Cart, for instance, is all about a prostitute. The Sanscrit poem called Naishada, or Nal Damayanti, now reprinting at a great expence in 22 cantos, is another of this nature. The whole object of the poet appears to be to display his critical acquaintance with the Sanscrit language and his exquisite taste for sensuality. At times, the author positively revels in licentiousness, and Don Juan is a tyro compared with him. The Committee will be able to judge of the character of the work when I inform them that the plot of the poem is as follows: Nala is rendered invisible and introduced by the god Indra into the harem of Damayanti to make love on his behalf to the beautiful mortal, but, as might have been expected, Nala fell in love himself and married the lady. A large portion of the poem is taken up in the detail of all that Nala observedi n the interior of the harem in the most unguarded hours of its inmates, while he himself preserved his invisible form. Repasts of this kind may contribute very much to the gratification of the oriental scholars of Europe and India. The book was of course intended exclusively for their perusal, and I strongly disclaim the idea of supposing that the members of the General Committee ever intended to pollute the minds of the youth of this country by teaching them lechery under its most seducive forms. These two books are only specimens of a great variety of the same character that might be named. If the sum which has been employed by the General Committee of Public Instruction in providing books for the amusement of oriental scholars in Europe, had been devoted to the supply of books of popular instruction, there would now be scarcely a school in the country which might not have been provided with some easy tracts of sound knowledge and pure morality. With the exception of the Sanscrit dramas, the works referred to are almost all quarto volumes, of seven hundred or eight hundred pages each, and, for the same cost at which one of these great books is got up, twenty or thirty, nay, sometimes eighty or a hundred school books, might be supplied.

Among other honours with which the administration of Lord William Bentinck will descend to posterity, it will not be the least, that in his time the Oriental mania, which broke out under Lord Wellesley's Government; advanced under Lord Minto's; was in the height of its career under Lord Hastings, and began to flag under Lord Amherst's; has completely exhausted itself. Orientalism has, at length, ceased to be considered the exclusive test of merit, and the public mind has completely awoke to the fact that the shortest and most effectual way of communicating knowledge to the people of this country is by educating the youth in English literature, and, where this is impracticable, by providing them with translations of books on European science in their own languages. All classes now concur in the expediency of opening in India the pure fount of English literature, and, where the parent source happens to be inaccessible to the student from the existence of other claims upon his time, he may at least be enabled to imbibe sound knowledge, though to a more limited extent, by means of translations in his native tongue.

According to the best of my judgment the truth lies in this opinion, but whether this be the case or not, it is certain that in proportion as the public have advanced towards this point, the majority of the Committee of Public Instruction have receded from it. By referring again to the annexed statement, it will be seen that in 1832 and 1833, seven Sanscrit and the same number of Arabic books were printed by the Committee and only one Hindee (which, like the others, was on an exclusively Sanscrit model) and none in Bengalee or Oordoo; while on the 2d November last, when the return was furnished, there were four Sanscrit and ten Arabic books in the press, and none in Hindee, Oordoo, or Bengalee. A change, therefore, has taken place, but it is all on the side of the learned languages and against popular instruction; and while Sanscrit used to be the principal object of the Committee's patronage, the tide has since turned in favour of Arabic. These learned languages seem to have just changed places in the estimation of the General Committee, and as there were 25 Sanscrit and 12 Arabic books published by them up to the end of 1831 and 1832, so there are now 10 Arabic and 4 Sanscrit books in the press; that is to say, while Sanscrit was formerly twice as much encouraged as Arabic, so now Arabic is twice as much encouraged as Sanscrit. In the year 1832 and 1833, the two languages were treated with equal favour, there having been exactly seven books published in each in that year. It will also be seen from the return that there are at this moment a number of translations into Arabic going through the press for the purpose of *popular* instruction, but there is no account of what they cost.

Compared with the limited use which can be made of them, owing to the small number of persons in India capable of reading and understanding Arabic books, the expence of these translations is very heavy. Indeed it is the rarity of acquirements like Mr. Tytler's, which is supposed to confer such a high value upon his labours. He is said to be the only person in India who is qualified for the task of translating English science into Arabic, from which we may form some conception of the limited number of individuals who possess such a practical acquaintance with this language as to render it easier for them to acquire knowledge through its medium than through that of any other. The Committee of the Agra College have for months past been advertizing for a native professor to fill the vacant chair in the department of Arabic Grammar, and no person possessing the necessary qualifications has yet made his appearance. The following is a statement of Mr. Tytler's receipts as Arabic translator general from September 1829 to March 1833:—

Works translated.	From what date.	Remuneration for Translation.			
Hooper's Vade Mecum	Sept. 1829. ...	1,000	0	0	
	Oct. " ...	1,000	0	0	
	Nov. " ...	1,000	0	0	
	Feb. 1830 ...	1,000	0	0	
	March " ...	1,000	0	0	
	April " ...	1,000	0	0	
	May " ...	1,000	0	0	
	July " ...	1,000	0	0	11 months at 742 Rs. per month.
		8,000	0	0	
Hutton's Mathematics, vol. 1st.......	Sept. " ...	1,000	0	0	
Crocker's Land Surveying...	Oct. " ...	1,000	0	0	2,000 Rs. 2 months at 1,000 Rs. per month.
Crocker's Land Surveying...	Nov. " ...	1,000	0	0	
	Jan. 1831 ...	1,000	0	0	2,000 Rs. 3 months at 666 10 8 ditto.
	May " ...	1,000	0	0	
Hutton's Mathematics.................	Sept. " ...	1,000	0	0	2,000 Rs. 5 months at 400 ditto.
Medical Books... ...	Ditto 1832 ...	750	0	0	
	Nov. " ...	750	0	0	
	Feb. 1833 ...	750	0	0	
	March " ...	750	0	0	3,000 Rs. 7 months at 428 9 ditto.

Abstract.

Remuneration received by Dr. Tytler for translating Hooper's Ana. Vade Mecum, ...	8,000
Ditto one-half Hutton's Mathematics, vol. 1st........	2,000
Ditto Crocker's Land Surveying	4,000
Ditto Hooper's Physician's Vade Mecum	3,000
	Rs. 17,000

Being 42 months at 400 Rs. a month.

This new light only lately broke in upon the majority of the General Committee, and it never seems to have been imagined before that translations into Arabic were good for public instruction. The prevailing taste used to be entirely on the side of Sanscrit. Brighter days, however, have at length begun to dawn upon India, and both Sanscrit and Arabic, after many a hard-fought battle, are slowly retiring from the field of popular education. The Arabic translations have been put a stop to, with the exception only of about 3,000 Rupees which were saved out of the fire, on the ground that Hooper's Anatomist's Vade Mecum was still incomplete. *At the period when this change took place* 65,000 *Rs. remained to be expended in completing Arabic translations of only six books, that is* 32,000 *Rs. for five Medical works, and* 33,000 *Rs. for the untranslated part of Hutton "with something extra for Diagrams."* This is according to Mr. Tytler's own estimate.

I am far from wishing to discourage the prosecution of oriental studies within their proper limits. If it be the duty of Government to preserve the knowledge of Sanscrit and Arabic as a branch of curious literary enquiry, after the public voice has decided against them as a medium of national instruction, let professorships be established and a certain portion of the public revenue set apart for this particular purpose; but let us not give out that we are instructing the people of India, while we are really only endeavouring to support our own reputation for oriental learning. If we were real *orientalists* we should make the welfare of *the East* the main object of our efforts and should endeavour to draw from the ample stores of Western learning intellectual food for the improvement of our Asiatic brethren, but our conduct is really exactly the reverse of this. Nothing effectual is done for popular education in the East. No efforts are made to naturalize in this country the knowledge which we have so largely to bestow and a considerable portion even of the scanty fund which has been assigned by the British Parliament for the purpose of Indian popular instruction, has been alienated by us to cater for the taste of the lovers of oriental learning in Europe. It seems to have been overlooked that the annual lakh of rupees was assigned by Parliament *for the education of the youth of India,* and that it was never intended from this source to provide matter for the lucubrations of Messrs. Bopp and Schlegel, or even to gratify the taste of the professors in the English Universities. However it may have been recognized elsewhere, I trust that the principles of the orientalists will not be admitted into our Committee, and that a book of popular instruction will not be rejected because it is suggested that its publication may "compromise our character with European scholars."

Mr. Tytler further observes, that Mr. Thompson's book appears to be "even below our general run of publications," and he adds that "it is a mere naked vocabulary destitute of every principle of scientific philology." These remarks afford a singular illustration of how diametrically opposite different people may think on the same subject. The very reasons for which Mr. Tytler objects to the book form the ground on which I have presumed to recommend it to the notice of the Committee. All the English and Oordoo Dictionaries which have yet been published are above both the comprehension and the purses of the people, and they are too scientific for their edification. They are inaccessible to the poor and unintelligible to the unlearned and to children. The lowest price at which Gilchrist's, Shakespear's, and the other existing English and Oordoo Dictionaries are to be obtained, places them beyond the reach of any except the highest class of the people, and they are often so much crowded with synonymes, drawn fresh from Arabic and Sanscrit, and quite unknown in common parlance, and contain such a profusion of learned etymologies as to puzzle and confound the minds of the uninitiated. Under these circumstances Mr. Thompson designed the plan of his "School Dictionary," intending to make it so cheap as to be within every body's reach, and so popular in its character as to be universally intelligible. The work has not been completed, and it is submitted to the Committee in the hope, that the author may be enabled through their assistance to bring it before the world. The price of each copy will be 4 Rupees, which is only one-fifth part of the cost of the Dictionaries hitherto published, and great care has been taken in the compilation of it to explain the meaning of the English words only by such synonymes as are in general use.

The existing Dictionaries have all been formed more or less

upon the Sanscrit, Arabic and Persian models, and their authors appear to have taken a pride in displaying their intimate acquaintance with barbaric lore. Their columns are swelled with foreign words, taken wholesale from Richardson and Wilson, without in the least considering whether or not they form part of the language of the country, and the general tendency to fall into this error has been greatly aggravated by the pedantic spirit of the native assistants of the lexicographers, who were almost always learned Mouluvees and Pundits, puffed up with literary pride and more conversant with musty volumes than with the spoken language of the land. Mr. Thompson's Dictionary, on the contrary, has been drawn up strictly on the popular model, and it has been steadily kept in view, as the main principle of the undertaking, to admit no word which is not in familiar use in the towns and villages of Upper India. "Scientific Philology" has been discarded from the work, *on principle,* and "popular philology" has been adopted in its room, and it is therefore as reasonable to expect that it should fail to conciliate the regard of the "man of letters," as that it should be accepted with pleasure by every one who considers the instruction of the many as an object of superior importance to the literary celebrity of the few. The education of the natives at large has too long been made a sacrifice to the exclusive taste of our orientalists, and philology, which is only one out of many branches of science, is the only one which has yet received any considerable cultivation in this country. We do not want a Babel of dead languages, but the living languages of the English and Indians. We do not want an ocean of words, but an influx of ideas.

In a late series of letters, signed with a German T. and published in the *India Gazette,* those persons who wish to encourage the Indians in their laudable endeavours to acquire our language, were taunted with the "extraordinary fact that amidst all the zeal at present manifested for teaching English no one step has been taken, either by individuals, or Societies, however much they profess to have the object at heart, for compiling either an English

Grammar or Dictionary for the use of the natives." An effort has now been made to supply one of these requisites; the step, the absence of which was lamented by the gentleman who designated himself by the German T., has been taken, and it was therefore reasonable to expect that Mr. Tytler, who evidently belongs to the same school with his German namesake, would have hailed the event with satisfaction and congratulated our Committee upon having provided a Dictionary which, although it did not come up to his standard of perfection, at any rate brought the means of learning English down to the level of every native, however narrow his circumstances might be; but instead of this, he condemned the work because it is "below our general run of publications" and because it would "compromise our character particularly with European scholars."

The same letter contains Mr. 𝕿.'s notion of a popular Dictionary which it will be useful to transcribe, as it furnishes a happy illustration of the motives which have induced his learned friend to reject Mr. Thompson's performance. "The Grammar must be accompanied by a copious Dictionary, comprising not a list of mere vocables, with a string of oriental words thrown after them in a random heap, but *a philosophical account of each word, explaining its etymology, its radical and metaphorical meanings* IN ALL THEIR SHADES, *its synonymes and cognates, its modes of construction, and the various idioms with which it is connected,* which in English are so numerous and so capricious, yet so necessary to be understood, the whole to be clothed in a simple style of *the native language which is that of* THE SCHOLARS, and *the points of similarity and difference between the English and oriental phraseology pointed out as they occur.*" The letter also contains a curious prospectus of a popular Grammar, but as it does not immediately relate to the subject before us, I will not allude to it further than by observing that it is worthy of perusal. A copy of the *India Gazette* containing Mr. 𝕿.'s letter is annexed to this paper.

Mr. Tytler states that the School Dictionary is a "mere naked vocabulary destitute of every principal of scientific philology," to which I fully assent, in the sense and for the reasons above stated; but then the learned gentleman goes on to say, "in which the words are thrown together in a heap" and "full of mistranslations and misapprehensions," which I deny. The term "thrown together in a heap" would lead one to suppose, that the Dictionary is of a complex character and that it is burdened with a number of useless synonymes, whereas the opposite to this is really the case. The plan of the work is of the simplest kind, and as no word has been introduced which is not in general use, the synonymes are very few. Generally speaking, there is only one, and there are seldom more than two or three. Any recourse to the Sanscrit or Arabic Dictionary was expressly excluded by the plan of the work, and there was, therefore, no source from which synonymes could be drawn except popular parlance.

The assertion that the book is "full of mistranslations and misapprehensions" could only be completely met by challenging an examination of it by a Committee of unprejudiced persons, which I should not hesitate to do, if the copyright belonged to me, which it does not. The book is the property of Mr. Thompson who depends in a great measure upon the produce of his literary labours for the means of providing for a numerous family, and I do not know how far he might be disposed to subject it to the risk of being condemned. He might think that the object to be attained by success would not compensate the loss which might ensue from defeat, because he could only gain the patronage of the School Book Society if the book were to be approved of, whereas he might lose not only their patronage, but the patronage of the public also by its formal condemnation. Perhaps also he might not place sufficient confidence in the gentlemen who have hitherto acquired a reputation as "great orientalists" to trust them with passing a decision upon the value of his property. It would at once occur to him that they would be likely to judge of his work by a standard which he does not acknowledge, and the language of Hindoostan is as yet so unfixed that if a work were ever so perfect, it might be condemned, according as one or another criterion might be adopted as the rule of decision. A lòver of Sanscrit might condemn it, because it did not sufficiently approach to the Sanscrit model. An Arabic scholar might object to it because many highly expressive words, which are probably in daily familiar use between the scholar and his moonshee, are omitted; while others are used in a sense in which they are not to be found in the original Arabic; and in the same way the Persian scholar might condemn it because the *thent* Hindee is sometimes preferred to a more elegant Persian synonyme. That such is not unlikely to be the case we have already had a convincing proof, since the moment the book came to Mr. Tytler, he condemned it because it had not been formed upon *his* model of "*scientific philology.*" There is a great difference also in the kind of Hindoostanee spoken at different places, and although the work might be perfectly identical with the language spoken at the majority of places and by the majority of persons in Upper India, it might differ greatly from that which is spoken at some places and by some persons. Sometimes Sanscrit, and sometimes Arabic and Persian, predominate in the language of different places and even of different persons in the same places; so that if Mr. Thompson did not happen to hit off that particular modification of the language with which the members of the examining Committee were familiar, he might be condemned, though entirely without fault, to lose the reward of all his labours. The Arabian Hindoostanee, which has grown up at Calcutta under the fostering patronage of Government and is spoken by the Moonshees of the College of Fort William and the Moulavees and students of the Mahomedan College, is quite a different language from that which prevails in any other part of India.

In judging of a work of this kind, a great deal must depend on the qualifications of the author and the character which he has at stake. Although he may not be known to all the members of the Committee, Mr. Thompson is a person of tried ability for the task which he has now brought to completion. He has resided for so many years in the Upper Provinces and has been brought by the nature of his duties into such frequent and familiar intercourse with people of all classes both in town and country, that he possesses a thorough acquaintance with the popular language, and besides this, he has had great experience in the preparation of books for the instruction of the people through his connection with the Serampore Mission. One of his last works was the Vocabulary to which the attention of the Committee has been already called. This little book is exactly on the same plan as the School Dictionary, only on a much smaller scale and, as before stated, it was the success attending this publication which encouraged Mr. Thompson to undertake the larger work. Owing to his reduced circumstances, he has not now the means of paying the expence of printing his Dictionary, and he therefore requests the assistance of the School Book Society, which, by taking a certain number of copies, may enable him to print the work, at the same time that the Society itself cannot be a loser by the transaction, as all the copies taken by it will readily sell at the price agreed on, or four rupees a copy, and the assistance given to him will therefore really be of the nature of an advance, to enable a deserving man to bring out a work of great popular utility. Mr. Thompson's letter is annexed, which will throw some additional light on the above remarks. For my part, I have spent some years in different parts of Upper India in constant communication with all classes of the people, and I can assure the Committee, that the School Dictionary contains the nearest approximation to the popular language which I have yet seen. No doubt it has some faults, like every other human production, but these may be rectified and great improvements may be made in subsequent editions.

(Signed) C. E. TREVELYAN.

Calcutta, January, 1834.

List of Books printed up to 30th April, 1833.

SANSCRIT.

	Copies	
Magdabódha	500	
Laghukáumudi	500	
Bháti Kávya, in 2 vols. 500 copies each	1,000	
Siddbánta Muktávali and Bhásha Pariochhéda	500	
Nayá Suttra Vati	500	
Sáhitya Darpana	500	
Védánta Sára	500	
Dáya Tatwá	500	Of these 250 copies each were given to the Editor for correcting proofs and collating.
Vyváhára Tatwá	500	
Dáya Krama Sangraha	500	
Dáyabhágha	500	
Mitákshára	560	
Manu Sanhitá, in 2 vols. 500 copies each	1,000	
Mrichchá Kati	500	Of this 100 copies each were given to the Editor for ditto ditto.
Uttára Ráma Charitra	500	
Vikrámaévasi	500	
Malaté Mádhava	500	
Mudvá Rashi	500	
Retnávalí	500	
Sanscrit and English Dictionary	500	
Lilávatí	500	
Raghu Vánsa	500	
Mahábhárata, vol. 1st	500	
	13,060	

ARABIC.

Majaz ul Qánún			300	
Sudídí			300	
Tashrih ul Qalb			500	
Fatáwá Alamgírí,	vol.	1st	500	
Ditto	ditto	2d	500	
Ditto	ditto	3d	500	
Ditto	ditto	4th	500	
Kifáyah	ditto	3d	500	Of these 250 copies each were given to the Editor for correcting proofs and collating.
Ditto	ditto	4th	500	
Ináyah	ditto	3d	500	
Ditto	ditto	4th	500	
Hidayah			500	Of this 100 copies ditto.
			5,600	

PERSIAN.

Lilávatí	500
Mulukhkhas ut Tuwarikh	500
Majmua Shamsi	500
Persian Miscellany	500
Esop's Fables	500
	2,500

HINDI.

Subhá Vilás	500
Rájníti	530
Chhatra Prakásá	500
Dáyabhágha	500
	2,030

ABSTRACT PRINTED.

Sanscrit	13,060
Arabic	5,600
Persian	2,500
Hindi	2,030
Total copies	23,190

In the Press.

SANSCRIT.

Mahábhárata, vol. 2d	500
Susrata	500
Ráj Tarangini	500
Naishadha	500

ARABIC.

Fatáwá Alamgírí, vol. 5th	
Anísul Mushárribín, Arabic Version of Hooper's Anatomist's Vade Mecum	500
Ustugisat, a treatise on Geometry	500
Jawámiá ilm-ur Riází, Arabic ditto of Hutton's Mathematics	500
Jawámiá ilm-ul Masáhat, Arabic ditto of Crocker's Land Surveyings	500
Bridge's Algebra, Arabic ditto	500

PERSIAN.

Harington's Analysis	500	
Khazánat ul Ilm	500	Of this 100 copies as above.

List of Books printed in 1832—33.

SANSCRIT.

Mahábhárata, vol. 1st.
Ráj Tarangini.
Retnávalí.
Naishadha.

HINDEE.

Dáyabhágha.

ARABIC.

Fatáwá Alamgírí, vol. 4 and 5; vol. 5, in the press.
Hidáyah.
Sadídí.

PERSIAN.

Khuzánat ul Ilm.

In the Press.

SANSCRIT.

Lilávatí.
Susrata.
Sanscrit and English Dictionary.

ARABIC.

Anís ul Mushárrihín.
Jawámiá ilm-ur Riází.
Jawámiá ilm-ul Musáhat.

Statement of Printing Charges.

Total charges of Printing from 1824-25 to 1829-30	69,347	2	4			
Deduct received from Mr. Pearce, by transfer of the printing materials	9,218	0	0	60,129	2	4
Total charges in 1830-31	19,363	8	9			
Ditto ditto 1831-32	16,653	6	3			
Ditto ditto 1832-33	7,103	11	9	43,120	10	9
				1,03,249	13	1
Add charges for printing Bridge's Algebra in the Bishop's College Press				2,176	0	0
Total				1,05,425	13	1

MR. PRINSEP'S MINUTE.

When on the first circulation of the proposal for subscribing to Mr. Thompson's Dictionary I recorded the minute which has been made the subject of so lengthened a reply from Mr. Trevelyan, I certainly never contemplated the probability of its forming the text of a voluminous disquisition in the *India Gazette*. In the ordinary business of a Committee consisting of about twenty members, little more than a vote or a brief remark could be allowed to each, or discussions would become interminable and real business would stand still. The broad questions and principles on which the education of the country should be conducted may form very proper themes for those who have the time and talent to write volumes upon them out of Committee. In it I think a contest of opinion would be very inconvenient, and I shall therefore merely trouble my brother Committeemen with a brief explanation of my former minute lest its purport should be misunderstood.

I said that a Vocabulary like Mr. Thompson's of Hindoostanee in Roman character would be much sought after by European students. I learned the spoken language thus myself, and I know how difficult it is, when such a text is available, to keep the eye upon the Native character. This was one motive for my objection. We print or purchase books (I presume) for schools of *Native youth*, not for European *educated adults*. In childhood it is equally easy to master either system, and it seems to me to be particularly desirable not to lose that opportunity of imprinting upon the pliable mind of the pupil, a thorough habit and facility of writing and reading his Native tongue; not to thwart his knowledge of it by keeping it out of sight, and pushing prominently forward a system which must keep him in comparative ignorance of the construction and orthography of his mother tongue. The only plea upon which Mr. Thompson's scheme could be upheld for *Native education,* is the eventual general substitution of the Roman character; which to me appears as chimerical as the establishment of an universal language or the "removal of the curse of Babel." At any rate a School Book Society of the present generation must conform to existing things, and give such books and such education as shall prove in after life to be most useful to its scholars. To a large class the knowledge of Persian and to a larger that of the Hindee is essential for the business of their lives, and it appears to me to be of much greater importance to ground them well in the *writing* of those languages (the speaking of them being their birthright cannot be eradicated though it may be systematized and purified) than even to introduce them to much vaunted English with all its moral and scientific advantages. The instruction of the country, as well as the business, and eventually the literature must be in the vernacular, and our aim ought to be to foster that, and transfuse into it the substance of our own advanced knowledge. Those whom we instruct in English are to be the pioneers and interpreters of this peaceful and insensible innovation, not the uncompromising guerillas of a violent and *ultra radical* subversion of all that now exists. What would the parents of a boy at the Calcutta Anglo-Indian College say if we turned out his son "a finished youth" without a knowledge of the Bengalee Alphabet? Have we yet seen a Bengalee Dictionary in the Roman character?

As for the superiority of English orthography I never heard a mother who did not complain of the difficulty of teaching a child the difference between C and S, and I will ask whether a Native child is more likely to learn the identity and the pronunciation of the word for "Town" from the unchangeable نگر or नगर, or from the delightfully variable nagar, nugur, nagore, nuggur, naghur, nigurh, nogor, and nugre, which will be naturalized by the introduction of the system Mr. Trevelyan advocates. For my part I think the urchin would as readily recognize the "City of God" *(Allahabad)* in the "isle of bats" and the Palace at Ghazeepore in "Chelsea tune" *(chuhul sitoon)*.

(Signed) J. PRINSEP.

2d January, 1834.

MR. TYTLER'S MINUTE.

In all this I fully CONCUR and feel much obliged to Mr. Prinsep for having expressed my sentiments so fully.

(Signed) J. T.

MR. TREVELYAN'S MINUTE.

I think it hard in Mr. Prinsep not to allow a large body of the youth of India the same advantage of learning Hindoostanee through the medium of the Roman letters, which he gratefully acknowledges in his own case. I repeat that there is a numerous class of Native youth rising in Upper India, who are acquainted only with the Roman characters; for their use Mr. Thompson's Vocabulary was prepared, and so highly was it appreciated by them, that the more extended plan of the dictionary was shortly after commenced upon. In assisting in the publication of Mr. Thompson's Dictionary, therefore, we are only conforming our operations to "the existing state of things" which is correctly stated by Mr. Prinsep to be the ruling principle of our society. Mr. Prinsep's mistake consists in his taking the last generation for the present, and he will not be persuaded that the people of this country have made such a considerable advance towards correct ideas as they really have.

But Mr. Prinsep would have them learn the Persian and Nagree characters at any rate, for the sake of enabling them to study *Hindoostanee literature.* I should like to know where this literature is to be found. I have never been able to discover it, unless such trash as the Khulela Dhumna and Bagho Behar, which are translations from the Persian got up by the Orientalists of Fort William, and a few popular songs can be called such. Miss Bird's books and a very few others which have been published in Hindoostanee of late years represent the whole body of the Hindoostanee literature, and I am prepared to have editions of them all printed in the Roman character, as soon as Mr. Thompson's dictionary is out. The truth is that we have to *construct a literature for Upper India from the beginning,* and the more we shut our eyes to the broad glare of this fact, the less disposed shall we be to enter upon our task with the zeal befitting its magnitude and importance.

Mr. Prinsep admits that in childhood it is *equally easy to master either system* of letters, and why, therefore, of the two systems, should we choose, in order to express the new literature, that which is the least perfect, and which will always render school books, one-third dearer than there is any necessity for owing to the superior cost of printing in Persian and Nagree. In my former minute, I endeavoured to prove that, as far as the Hindoostanee language is concerned, every object of "construction and orthography" is more effectually answered by the use of the Roman than of the Persian letters, and that with regard to the question between the Roman and *Nagree* letters, these ends are at least equally answered by both, but without replying to my arguments, Mr. Prinsep has now made a contrary assumption.

But "construction and orthography" are only a very insignificant part of the question. The object of language is to impart knowledge and whence is this to be derived, for the Hindoostanee language does not contain it at present in any recorded shape? Mr. Prinsep would marry the Hindoostanee to the Persian language by maintaining the Persian character for both and encouraging the study of the Persian language; while I, on the other hand, would form a close union between the *English* and Hindoostanee by using the English character for both, and encouraging the study of the English language. The beau ideal of a place of education according to the gentlemen who think with Mr. Prinsep, is the Mahomedan College, where the youth of India are bribed, by the offer of excessive emoluments, to imbibe systems of error, which we all know have been exploded, and their falsehood demonstrated ages ago. The astronomy of Ptolemy, the medicine of Galen and Hippocrates, and the logic of Aristotle! Although we should scorn the idea of English youth being even permitted to waste their time upon such studies, yet the children of this country are not only allowed to do so, *but extraordinary advantages are offered to those who can be induced through the influence of such motives to devote the best years of their lives to them.* A system of education which we should never for a moment think of using ourselves is considered quite good enough for our Indian fellow-men and fellow-subjects. I will never cease to protest against this wilful murder of the minds and time of the youth entrusted to our charge. Was there ever such a thing heard of in any other country in the world as that *rewards should be held out for the propagation of falsehood far exceeding in liberality any that are offered for the cultivation of truth?* At the Mahomedan College the youth are seduced into the study of Ptolemy's Astronomy by a bribe which costs the state more than 30 Rs. a month, while, at the Hindoo College, they get nothing for studying Newton and have to pay besides! I have often admired the good sense of the Hindoo community of Calcutta who long ago rejected the absurd system of education which the then existing Government held out for their acceptance and established the Hindoo College at their own expense.

Mr. Prinsep says with great propriety, "those whom we instruct in English are to be the pioneers and interpreters of this peaceful and insensible invasion." The natives of the country, those whose mother tongue the vernacular idioms are, must be the translators, the noble artificers of the literature which will hereafter constitute the medium through which the treasures of knowledge will be laid open to the mass of their countrymen. A moderate acquaintance with a foreign tongue suffices to enable a person to collect the sense which is to be translated; but a far more perfect knowledge of a language than a foreigner is generally able to acquire is necessary to write successfully in it.

So far Mr. Prinsep and myself are quite agreed, but then comes the question how the future translators are to acquire such a taste for science and such an acquaintance with its principles as will qualify them for the great work in which they are to be engaged. Mr. Prinsep would have them *all taught Persian*, but, unless it be intended to contaminate the popular languages with such polluted streams as the Mahomedan College youths are taught to rejoice in, which is not the case, I cannot imagine how this plan can forward the end in view. The youth cannot learn *two* foreign languages. Even in England where the state of society admits of more leisure and consequently of education being carried further than is the case in this country, not one young man in a thousand obtains a tolerable acquaintance with more than one foreign language, and in India, where fathers are generally anxious to put their sons out in life at 16, it is quite out of the question. They cannot be expected to learn both Persian and English. To which therefore are they to be encouraged to give their attention in preference? Mr. Prinsep says Persian. I say English. Translations of books on European science are every day put forth by the young men who have been educated at the Hindoo College, and let Mr. Prinsep point out a single such translation which has been accomplished by a person educated principally at the Mahomedan College where Persian and English are joined in monstrous connection. As Persian and Arabic literature form the principal subject of their studies, this class of people do not possess the necessary qualifications to become translators of European science. They are only able tō propagate the corrupt and erroneous Persian system by means of such translations as the Khulela Dhumna and Bagho Behar.

It is quite a mistake to suppose that a knowledge of Persian is "essential for the business of the lives" of the rising generation. The only reason why English does not at once take the place of Persian in the Courts of Justice and other offices of Government is, because a sufficient number of persons qualified in the English language are not at present procurable. Those fathers who are so besotted as to teach their children Persian will hereafter lament the inferiority of their own offspring to the children of their neighbours who had sense enough to perceive the signs of the times and to give their sons an English education, and they will grieve at the recollection of the invaluable years, never to be recovered, which have been thrown away in studying a language the learning of which is a system of error; the style of which is so depraved and servile as to be quite unfit to form an habitual medium for the expression of the sentiments of British subjects, and in favor of which the utmost that can be said is that it is spoken in Persia, and contains some pretty poetry, which for the most part is very immoral. The recommendation that it is necessary for the transaction of business only applies to those who are now practising in the Courts. Five years hence the case will be very different, and instead of being considered as a qualification, the very reverse will be the case. It will be regarded as a strong presumption against the general fitness of a person for office that he has had a Persian education, and I should not wonder if *farseedan* (a knower of Persian) were to grow into a byword and stigma before ten years pass over our heads.

I beg leave to call the attention of the Committee to what Mr. Prinsep calls "the unchangeable نگر." Now let us consider in how many ways this unchangeable combination of letters can be pronounced نُگِر نُگَر نِگُر نَگُر نِگَر نَگَر nugur, nigar, nugir, nugoor, nigoor, noogur, noogir, and so forth. And I contend that *nugur* deserves the epithet of "unchangeable" much better than this. From a reference to Mr. Thompson's scheme of vowels it will be seen that in his book *u* is *invariably* used as in *purse*, and, when the system comes more into vogue, the same uniform plan, or another equally good, will be pursued. The Sanscrit is a better character than the Persian, but it is much less known to the class of Native youth in Upper India who will use Mr. Thompson's Dictionary than the English is; besides which, I must recall the attention of the Committee to the strange and unaccountable notion of forcing another character besides the Roman into the Dictionary when it is not in the least required for the assistance of the Student. He must read the English column in Roman characters at any rate, and if he has a sufficient acquaintance with them to be able to do this, he will of course be able to read his own language in the same characters with much greater facility.

An apology is due from me to the Committee for taking up so

much of their time. The serious importance of the subject is my excuse, and I hope it will be deemed sufficient.

(Signed) C. E. TREVELYAN.

February 4th, 1834.

MR. TYTLER'S REPLY TO MR. TREVELYAN.

To the Editor of the India Gazette.

SIR,

I am not fond of professed newspaper controversy. I engage in it now, as thinking that, besides what is due to myself, something also is due the Committee of the School Book Society in explanation of that minute of mine respecting Mr. Thompson's English and Oordoo Dictionary, which is commented on at so much length in your papers of January 28th and 29th. Had this comment been confined to my opinion given in to the Society, I should have replied to it only in the regular circulation of the Society's box, but as it has a reference also to my employments under the Committee of Public Instruction and to a variety of extraneous matter besides, it becomes necessary for me to adopt another mode of communicating my sentiments. Want of time prevented my doing this sooner.

I shall begin by observing that the minute in question was communicated by me to the members of the School Book Society in confidence: I had not the least idea of its ever going further, and do not see what advantage can accrue to any party from its publication.

I shall not enter here into the merits of Mr. Thompson's work, but confine myself to a brief consideration of a few of the other topics touched on in Mr. Trevelyan's minute.

The first of these is the revival of the old project for printing Oriental books in Roman characters. Most people, I believe, supposed that after the ponderous volumes on this subject with which Dr. Gilchrist so long afflicted the public, the subject had been pretty well set at rest, and that the worthy Doctor had fully succeeded in demonstrating the utter impossibility of his own system. As, however, it appears that the plan is proposed to be revived, and the School Book Society are called upon publicly, and upon principle to grant their approbation and patronage to works thus formed, it becomes my duty, as a member of the Society, to enquire how far they are likely to advance their own reputation, or to benefit the public by so doing.

I shall admit thus much, that a short Vocabulary of the kind may be useful enough to a fresh arrived Griffin in enabling him to give a few common orders to his servants; but surely this is not a want which the School Book Society was instituted to supply.

The printing of Oriental books in Roman character must be either to enable Europeans more easily to learn the Oriental languages, or to enable Orientals to read them with more facility.

As to the first of those objects: I should ask, upon what principle can it rationally be expected that a person who has not perseverance enough to learn the *letters* of a language should ever be able to learn *the language itself*. We might as reasonably propose carrying a student through the Principia who declared himself unable to master the multiplication table. The letters are most assuredly the easiest part of every language, and he who declares himself willing to learn the rest, though he cannot or will not learn these, in truth declares that though he is not able to lift five seers, he is yet quite willing and capable to lift five hundred.

Next, as to the advantages which the Orientals are to derive from this scheme: it is certain that of all the parts of our language its alphabet is the most unfortunate to select as fit for transplantation to the East; since, however much and however justly we may admire the other properties of the English tongue, it is utterly impossible to admire its orthography. Our alphabet is at once so redundant and deficient, so barbarous and unscientific, that its substitution for the Arabic or Sanscrit, far from being an advance in intellect, would be a decided retrogression. For this the reason is easily assigned. The European alphabets have not, like European sciences, been formed and successively improved through a long course of ages of increasing intelligence: they were formed in times of the darkest ignorance, and have remained unchanged and unimproved since then. They are, as might be expected, radically imperfect; and to add to the confusion, while the pronunciation of European languages has gone on altering, the orthography for the last three hundred years has remained nearly unchanged. The consequence of all is, that the spelling of English and French at least, is so capricious, and the words written bear so little resemblance to the words pronounced, that no one could tolerate our orthography but those to whom it has been familiar from their cradle; and in fact any unprejudiced person taking up Walker's Dictionary and comparing the written with the pronounced words, will find scarcely a single letter in all our Christ Cross Row of which the sound is ascertained, and will be apt to think our system more allied to Chinese arbitrary marks than to alphabetic spelling.*

It is certainly extremely difficult to see what advantage the Natives can derive from having a system forced upon them so imperfect and so much less precise than their own.

Besides, there are a number of sounds in the Oriental languages which no Roman letters and no combination of Roman letters can express, and which no two persons will agree in their mode of representing. The whole question, then, may be dismissed as an unprofitable discussion, till it be decided according to what system the Oriental words are to be written. Without this it is odds that if twenty different books were printed by as many persons, almost each word would be found spelt in twenty different ways, not one expressing the true sound. The sum of the whole is, that our let-

* Instances of this are too familiar to require enumeration, but we may take as an example the words rite, write, right, wright, which all have the same sound, but whose spelling sets system at defiance.

ters were never intended for their languages, and therefore cannot express their sounds.*

In what Mr. Trevelyan says of the Greek and German and Russian alphabets, he confounds two things essentially different; —the shape of the letters and the system of the alphabet; the one a matter of very little importance, the other the whole basis of the dispute. The English printed and written characters, their capitals and their small letters, are all different; yet it will not be affirmed that they are different alphabets; they are all formed on the same system and represent the same sound. In the same manner, though the Roman, the German, and the Greek, (I am not acquainted with the Russian), are a little different in shape, the principal, and by far the majority of sounds in all, are the same; and it is a matter of little consequence whether to express the same

---

* I shall here support myself by the authority of the "master of thirty legions." In a list of native names now before me, issued from the Adjutant General's Office, I find the simple appellation علی expressed in the following modes, Ali, Allee, Ullee, Allie. And in the same way another word thus :. Shekh, Shaickh, Shaick, Sheick, Shaikh, Shaik: which of these is to be adopted in our Roman Oriental alphabet? Not one of them expresses the right sound except the last but one, Shaikh, and that will only do so by giving kh a sound which it never has in English, that is of ch in the Scotch Loch, Buchan, or in the German Buch, and which no doubt is that of the Greek X. I shall also mention another authority, who is not, I think, altogether to be despised. Not knowing whether Mr. Trevelyan ranks French in the class of barbarous and unintelligible languages, I shall venture to leave it untranslated. "On s'est fié á l'oreille, en apprenant les noms de la bouche des naturels du pays; mais l'oreille saisit mal les sons d'une langue inconnue. Ensuite on a voulu exprimer ces sons par la valeur que les lettres Latines ont dans la langue Anglaise; et c'est lá une enterprise *impossible et contradictoire en elle même.* L'orthographie ou plutôt la *scoliographie* Anglaise n'a rien à démêler avec la prononciation; elle est historique, elle désigne la prononciation d'un autre temps, altérée depuis. Beaucoup de lettres ne sont pas prononcées du tout; plusieurs consonnes ont un son différent selon les mots où elles sont employées. Deux voyelles homogênes significant souvent une voyelle différente, et des voyelles simples une dipthongue; d'autres dipthongues ou voyelles longues sont exprimées par la réunion d'une voyelle et d'une semi consonne. D'ailleurs la langue Anglaise d'aujourd'hui abonde en voyelles qui n'ont pas de place bien fixe dans l'échelle musicale des sons articulés.—*Schlegel's Reflexions sur l'étude des langues Asiatiques addressées á Sir James Mackintosh.*

sound we employ P, 𝔓, or Π ; L, 𝔏, or Λ. The same parallelism, however, by no means exists in the European and Oriental alphabets. The Oriental alphabets are not, like the European, *literal*,—they are *syllabic ;* that is, each element expresses not a simple sound, but a syllable. In English, for example, no consonant can be pronounced without the addition of a vowel. In Arabic and Nagree, on the contrary, each letter is a consonant with a vowel inherently combined : to use it as a simple consonant a mark must be added, indicating that the vowel is taken away. Which of those two systems is the best, is a question that would admit of long discussion : each no doubt, has its advantages and disadvantages. It is plain, however, that we are not to take it for granted that ours is the best, merely because it is that to which we are accustomed.

Mr. Trevelyan asserts that "the old German text is now almost entirely abandoned, and few new books are published in Germany except in the Roman character." On what he founds this assertion I am at a loss to know. I certainly was not aware of the fact as he states it : I have now before me (not a very old nor unpopular book) Goëthe's Wilhelm Meister, published in the usual German character at Stuttgard in 1816, and by going into another room I could collect forty or fifty volumes of the same kind; while, I believe, I have not above two or three in the Roman : Mr. Trevelyan will also find abundance of modern German periodicals in the Asiatic Society's Library. To settle this point, however, at once, I shall bring forward a more satisfactory authority than any in this country can be. "For this reason, many German works have, in more recent times, been printed in Roman type : that practice, however, is hitherto not become general, and the greatest number of publications continues to appear in the ancient habit ; and it is to be doubted whether that innovation would be of any advantage, if generally adopted. By disaccustoming the eye from the old type, many valuable productions of literature, unless reprinted, would be rendered less easy to read, and might be prejudiced in their general utility. Of late years, however, the disposition of disusing the character, and substituting for it the Roman letter, instead of increasing, has considerably diminished; and I believe I am right in asserting, that *now by far the greatest number of German books is printed in the old type.*"—*G. H. Noehden's German Grammar, fifth edition*, 1827, pp. 18, 19.

A few miscellaneous observations are to be made on the advantages which it is stated would result from using Roman characters. One is, that the vowels are expressed "instead of being either entirely omitted, (in the Oriental alphabets) or distinguished by diacritical* points." This is the case only to a very partial extent. It is but the short vowels that are omitted in Hebrew, Arabic, and Persian, the long are all expressed. Both long and short are very accurately expressed in the Nagree and its derivative alphabets. On the other hand, the Roman alphabet labours under the great disadvantage that it has no distinction between long and short vowels, and this in the accurate writing of words, far more than counterbalances all the difficulties of the Oriental orthography.† I omit the perfectly capricious and unaccountable manner in which the vowels and diphthongs and triphthongs are pronounced in English, as these must be obvious to every one, and are past defending.‡

With respect to the superior distinctness of the Roman letters,

---

* Strictly speaking, *diacritical* points are the dots which distinguish several letters of the Arabic and Persian Alphabets. The marks for the short vowels zubur, zere, peshe, are *vowel* points.

† What, for example, must a native medical student think of our orthography when he is taught to pronounce the o in Camphora and Cinchona so differently, or the *i* in Serratus Anticus, and Flexor Pollicis. If, to remedy this, we employ the prosodial marks of longs and shorts, this is the system of diacritical points which Mr. Trevelyan so much condemns.

‡ English, it is known, wants the sound of the Italian and German u, that is the Persian peshe and the 5th Nagree vowel: this is a great defect which our attempts to remedy have been very unsuccessful. We employ at least ten different combinations of vowels to express a sound in itself perfectly simple. Thus o, u, eu, ew, oe, oo, ou, ough, ue, wo, as in these words: to, flute, feud, new, shoe, too, soup, through, sue, two. There may be more that I don't recollect: the pronunciation of *e* defies all classification.

I must say this advantage appears to me wholly imaginary. No doubt in the books printed twenty or thirty years ago the characters were very indistinct, chiefly I believe, from an injudicious wish of closely imitating the written hand. Since, however, that idea has been abandoned* and our books have been printed in the niskhee character, they have every year improved, and I cannot be persuaded that any one can find the least difficulty in reading the Arabic and Nagree typography of Mr. Pearce.† He who cannot learn these, must, I think, be unable to learn any characters at all. Besides, there is no reason why we should not go on if necessary in our improvements in the Oriental *printed* letters, and form, in comparatively a very few years, a set of characters even more distinct than we have now.

Again: Mr. Trevelyan states that printing can be carried on in Roman characters much cheaper and more expeditiously than in Persian or Nagree. This would be incontrovertible did the same number of Roman as of Oriental letters serve to express a given word. Every one, however, who has tried knows, that to express a given Oriental word requires many more Roman than Oriental letters; and conversely, to express the generality of European words, more Oriental than Roman characters are necessary. This

---

* The chief supporter of this plan was Dr. Lumsden; at least he mentions it, seemingly with approbation, in his preface to his edition of the first volume of the Shah Nameh. Of its disadvantages any one may convince himself in a moment, by comparing the broken and confused letters in that volume, with the distinct and elegant typography in Captain Macan's noble edition of the same work.

I may observe, that for this great improvement in typography, I mean the distinction between the written and printed character, we are, I imagine, mainly indebted to the meritorious exertions of Dr. Rind. The honour of establishing the first Lithographic Press in India belongs to that Gentleman. Before his time we had no cheap way of giving any idea of the written character except through types, which it was necessary therefore to make so as to resemble manuscript: but that invaluable invention enables us now to copy any characters we please; and we can accordingly employ Lithography when it is necessary to publish works in the *written* character, reserving our types to express the niskhee or printed.

† The Natives consider some of Mr. Pearce's types so beautiful that, as he has informed me, they declared nothing should be printed by them but the Koran.

is a general principle through all parts of language : every translation comprehends more words than its original. The letters of one language will not answer for those of another formed on a different system, and the words are never precisely parallel, to render them so, something explanatory must always be added. In attempting to write an Oriental language then in Roman letters, a great deal of room must be taken up, and the compositor's work increased. I am not prepared to say that this will actually make the Roman books dearer than the Oriental, but it will certainly much diminish their cheapness.*

It is easy no doubt to call the Nagree and Arabic characters "barbarous :" that is an epithet with which all nations have been in the habit of honouring each other since the beginning of time, and generally those who have most deserved it, have been most liberal in its application.† The Mouluvees and Pundits have only to bestow, as no doubt they do, the same appellation upon our alphabets, and the argument is equal on both sides. But these surely are unfit expressions to be brought into a literary discussion :

---

* To shew this I shall take the first book that comes in my way—the opening sentence of Syud Auzumooddeen's English Grammar.

چون ظاهراست که درزمان قلیل زبان فارسي ازتمام
هندوستان رخصت خواهد شد لهذا *

Choon zauhir ast keh dur zumaun e quleel zoobaun e Faursee az tumaum e Hindoostaun rookhsut khwahid shud lehauza.

"As it is self-evident that in a short time the Persian language is to bid good bye to the whole of Hindoostan, therefore"—

I cannot be accused of having employed too many characters ; yet on counting it will be seen that to express 60 Persian, 94 Roman must be employed ; that is more than one and a half for one. An inspection of this book will shew that to complete the scheme, it seems proposed to teach the Natives English in the *Persian* character, so that each language is to be disguised interchangeably in the letters of the other. This will no doubt be a vast step in the march of intellect.

† "God curse these dogs, what a strange barbarous language they speak !"—*Gibbon*, chap. 51, A. D. 638. Such was the judgment of a conqueror on the language of Homer. The old Sclavonians, not understanding the language of foreigners, modestly concluded that all mankind but themselves were dumb.

they do little honour to the party using them, and are not likely to produce much conviction in the mind of his antagonist. No one who contemplates the ingenuity of the Arabic and Sanscrit orthography, will be induced to bestow such an epithet on the noblest invention of the human mind.

Leaving this, however, as a matter of taste in argumentation, I shall go on to notice that Mr. Trevelyan speaks of "the many barbarous characters with which the country abounds." He surely must know that, with the exception of Arabic, they are all derived from Nagree, and in most cases with so little variation that any one who has mastered that, (which he may do in a week) may learn any other he chooses in three days, and at any rate, no one, I presume, unless he likes, need learn them all. One or two is generally sufficient for useful purposes. The difference between the various Hindoo alphabets is certainly not much greater than between our Roman and Italian, Writing and Old English characters,* Capitals and Smalls, to say nothing of Greek, which altogether compose eight distinct and very dissimilar alphabets as far as the shapes of the letters go.

To use Mr. Trevelyan's own words, "it is shocking to think how much human time, which may be directed to the best purposes, is wasted in gaining a knowledge of the barbarous characters with which the British islands abound"—with this additional grievance, that in Europe our unfortunate infants are compelled to learn them all, while the happier youth of Hindostan have seldom to learn more than one.

Admitting, however, the inconvenience to be as great as Mr. Trevelyan states, it is difficult to understand how this would be remedied by adding to the number, and bringing in upon the Na-

* The reading of all these is not to be considered a matter of no moment: it is recorded to the honour of Johnson's first schoolmistress that she could do so. "He was," says Boswell, "first taught to read English by Dame Oliver, a widow, who kept a school for young children in Lichfield. He told me she could read the black letter, and asked him to borrow for her, from his father, a Bible in that character."—*Boswell's life in the beginning.*

tives a set of new characters totally incongruous and immiscible with the old. Mr. Trevelyan will not, I suppose, go the length of saying that the Natives are to be prohibited by a regulation of the Governor General in Council, from using their own alphabets in their letters and private concerns; and as long as they continue to do so,—which will, in all probability, be longer than any of the present generation will have an opportunity to witness,—so long will the Roman printed books instead of diminishing, add inconceivably to the confusion.

It is not to be denied, however, that diversity of alphabets is, to a certain extent, an evil which it would be desirable to remedy, and the plan which the Committee of Public Instruction have gone upon, is as rational as any that can be devised. It is, to fix on some well known, distinct, and easily learnt character and employ that universally in printing. The Deb Nagree immediately suggests itself as that which of all others possesses these characteristics, and it is in that accordingly that the Committee's books are printed. This imposes on the Bengal, Tamool, or Orissa readers a task no greater, nor even so great, as to an Englishman that of learning the German letters after knowing the Roman or Italian, and this is surely not much to be complained of.

Still, the whole subject has, I think, been invested with a disproportionate degree of importance, and the mole-hill in some measure exalted into a mountain. After all, the letters, as was said before, are the easiest part of every language: he who will not learn them, certainly will not learn the rest, and I cannot be persuaded that the bare learning of an alphabet is such a heavy imposition on youths of common capacity. On the contrary, I think a knowledge of different alphabetic systems is *primâ facie* likely to be very beneficial in enlarging their views and improving their capacity.

Mr. Trevelyan thinks that it would be desirable "to engraft upon the popular languages of the East such words as *virtue, honour, gratitude, patriotism, public spirit,* and some others, for which it is at present difficult to find any synonyme in them."

To me, on the contrary, it appears that the bare engrafting of these words would be a matter of very little moment; it would only be a part of the system of teaching words instead of things, which unhappily prevails so much throughout Indian education. If indeed, we could infuse into the breasts of the Natives the *ideas* expressed by these words, this, I am willing to allow would be a real benefit,* but the bare teaching them the words is a very short step towards this object. Could we really succeed in teaching the virtues, we might safely leave the invention of the proper terms to the Natives themselves; and whether in this case they were taken from a European or Oriental source, is scarcely worth while to consider.

It may be right that I should here take some notice of the Delhi College which is spoken of so highly. Having no knowledge of its constitution, except what Mr. Trevelyan's minute affords, I can, of course, only speak from what appears there. I think it might be prudent to be moderate in its eulogiums till we see what sort of scholars it produces, and this more especially as the Allahabad school, of which we heard so much sometime ago, has been, I am told, a complete failure. If it be really the case, as Mr. Trevelyan informs us, that the pupils of the Delhi College "have no acquaintance whatever either with the Nagree or Persian character. They know English as their language of education, and Hindostanee as their vernacular tongue; but the only character with which they are acquainted is the Roman, and this they employ to write both languages," one can scarcely conceive more helpless members of society than they must ultimately turn out, nor a system of education less likely to benefit its alumni. What would be thought of a proposal at home to teach English through the medium of the Persian characters? Yet this, disguise it from

* I say this to avoid the appearance of cavilling, but to confess the truth, there are more than one in Mr. Trevelyan's list of virtues which appear to me very suspicious. For the whole I would venture to substitute, The Love of God and the Love of Man.

ourselves as we will, is the plan on which, by Mr. Trevelyan's account, the Delhi College is proceeding. No doubt its success is possible, but the best disciple of De Moivre would be puzzled to calculate the infinitely small chances in its favour. All we can do is to hope that the pupils steal a march on their teachers, and learn in secret the characters which are prohibited to them publicly, so that at their coming out into the world they may be able to read and write like their countrymen.

Mr. Trevelyan tells us that the vernacular language of the Delhi students is Hindostanee. It would be desirable to know what that language is: the Natives are quite unacquainted with it,—*they know no such language as Hindostanee.* It is a word entirely grown up among Europeans, to supercede the old and elegant appellation of Moors, which is still to be found in the mouths of some Indians of the olden time. What Europeans mean by it, is I believe, the Rekhtu or Oordhoo. Now this Rekhtu is composed (like English) from three sources, Arabic, Persian, and the old Hindee, which last may be the mother, sister, or daughter of Sanscrit. But there is this difference, that Arabic and Persian enter into Rekhtu in a much greater proportion than either Latin or French into English. To talk, then, of using Hindostanee and abandoning Arabic and Persian, is a plain contradiction in terms; and if Rekhtu be the language, (as no doubt it is) of the Delhi students, they must be, at this moment, using a large proportion of those very languages which Mr. Trevelyan pronounces dead, barbarous, and unintelligible.*

---

* I draw this conclusion chiefly from Mr. Thompson's book, which Mr. Trevelyan tells us is intended for the Delhi pupils. A large proportion of its Vocables are pure Persian and Arabic. I do not mention this as matter of blame. From the nature of the language it must be so.

In general, in Hindostanee the substantives are purely Persian and Arabic, and the verbs derivations with some alterations from Sanscrit. To give an idea of how those are combined, I shall take the first and most simple of the "Pleasant Stories" contained in the first volume, p. 344, of the Hindostanee Selections used at the College of Fort William, and substitute in it French words for Persian, Latin for

It is worthy of remark also, that the plan of having one vernacular and one language for education is by no means well calculated for mental improvement; because it completely separates the objects of education from the affairs of common life. It was this,

---

Arabic, and mark the Sanscrit derivatives by printing them in capitals. The story, (and its style cannot be called very complicated) is as follows:

It is UNDERSTOOD that A *quidam* WENT to a certain *monarque* and BEGAN to MAKE *prætentionem de l' inspiration*. *Le monarque ordonna* that *opus est miraculi* to *un prophete*. Do thou, SHEW one. HE REPLIED I WILL DO whatever you TELL me, for I am *prophete*. At that *tempus* there was an IRON *claustrum* in the HAND of *le monarque*. He SAID *si* thou art *prophete*, OPEN THIS. HE REPLIED, I MADE *prætentionem de l' inspiration* and not *d'etre forgeron*. At this saying, he BEGAN to LAUGH, and having GIVEN (a present) MADE *missionem*.

Can it, I would ask, be reasonably said, that such a composition as this could be understood by those utterly ignorant of French and Latin, or that either of these languages was dead in a country where such a dialect formed the vernacular speech. Yet such is exactly the case with what is called Hindostanee.

In the same manner to shew the connection between Bengalee and Sanscrit, I shall take a paragraph from the translation of the abridgement of Dr. Goldsmith's History of Greece by Khettro Mohun Mookerjea, which having been printed under the patronage of the School Book Society, and excessively praised by all the newspapers of the time, is to be considered, I suppose, quite classical: the passage I have taken is this :—

"To counteract, however, the influence of a popular assembly, Solon gave greater weight to the Court of Areopagus, and also instituted another council consisting of four hundred. Before his time the Areopagus was composed of such citizens as were most remarkable for their probity and wisdom. But Solon now ordained, that none should be admitted into it but such as had passed through the office of Archon."

The following is a re-translation of the Bengalee into English, in which Latin words are substituted for Sanscrit: it will appear that they are, if possible, even of more frequent occurrence than the Arabic and Persian in Oordhoo.

Sed thus *potentia* of the *populus* could not receive *magnam augmentationem*,* with this *consilium* Solon bestowed *ingens onus administrationis* on the *conventus judiciarius nomine* Areopeg; and besides this he caused *alter conventus consiliarius* to be *constitutus*, in which there were four hundred *consiliarii*. *Ante tempus administrationis Solonis, universi cives*,* who on account of their *fidelitas* and *sapientia* had obtained *famam*, composed *conventum* of the Areopeg *sed tempore administrationis Solonis*; this was the *mos** that none but those who had performed the *munus* of Archon could be *conjunctus* with this *conventus*.—p. 24.

Such is the style of the Bengalee translations, which it is said are to be encour-

by universal confession, that kept Europe so long in a state of ignorance during the middle ages: all science was taught in Latin, while the people were speaking the modern tongues. The consequence was, no knowledge ever diffused itself among them, and whatever existed, remained shut up in the walls of the College.

The great objections indeed to the exclusive use of English in education is, that it necessarily discourages the Natives from the cultivation of their own tongues. It puts an end to Native composition and indigenous literature, and confines their whole efforts to a wretched and servile imitation of English models, than which nothing can possibly have a greater tendency to prevent improvement. As long as European literature was confined to Latin the attempts of our ancestors at composition, the far greater part of which are now deservedly forgotten, were forced imitations of the Classics. Their philosophy was nothing more than a jejune commentary on the imperfect system of the ancients, and their poetry, a cento in which the lines and half lines of the classical masters, taken from their original situations, are forced into new and unnatural combinations. So it will be with the English productions of the Natives of India: their prose will be a mere patchwork of sentences extracted from the common-place English books with which they are acquainted, destitute of any effort of original thought, and their verse a bald imitation of Thomas Moore and Lord Byron. Such productions Europeans may now agree to praise and call wonderful specimens of Native poetic talent, but

---

aged as being simple and intelligible. He who can understand the above without Latin will understand Bengalee without Sanscrit. It is worthy of remark, that short and easy as is this passage, there are in it three mistranslations marked by asterisks. The first is directly opposite to the original, which implies that there was danger, lest the power of the people should become too great: the Bengalee translation implies, that it could not become great enough. In the second, the original is, that the members of the Areopagus were chosen out of those eminent for probity and wisdom. The translation is, that all the men of probity and wisdom that could be found in the city formed the Areopagus. In the third, the original has it that Solon made a law: the translation states that a custom existed in Solon's time. How can we expect the Natives to learn from works so incorrect as this?

the next generation will assuredly reject them with astonishment that they were ever esteemed. All this, so far from enlarging the ideas, is the most effectual means of cramping the intellect and keeping it in perpetual trammels.

I now come to that part of the Minute which more especially applies to myself; and to prevent all misapprehension and appearance of self-contradiction, shall here endeavour to state clearly my opinion of Oriental literature, and the uses to which it may be applied.

The first part of my literary creed, then, is this. Without denying that occasional scintillations of genius appear in the poetry and romances of the East, still I hold that they are greatly inferior to those of the West, and I also hold that Eastern sciences bear scarcely more proportion to those of Europe, than the first lispings of an infant to the ratiocinations of a man.

If it then be enquired, what is gained by the study of Oriental literature?—the answer divides itself into two parts:—first, the speculative; next, the practical. The speculative advantages are those which a person of a contemplative and inquiring turn of mind derives from that most delightful of all purely mental pleasures, an increase of knowledge. In the present case the student of the Oriental languages enlarges his views as to the structure of language, the history and antiquities of nations, the sentiments of mankind in different ages and under different circumstances. As long as human nature is what it is, these subjects will continue to be interesting; and he who attempts to blot them out from our view, so far from improving does what he can to degrade and dishonour our species.

Besides this, though Oriental science is very inferior, I am by no means disposed to admit that it is worth nothing at all: many valuable hints may be gained from the labours of our predecessors, and many useful lessons learnt from their mistakes. The history of science is in many cases almost as useful as science itself. "There is no part of history so generally useful as that which relates to the progress of the human mind, the gradual improvement of reason, the successive advantages of science, the vicissitudes of learning and ignorance, which are the light and darkness of thinking beings, the extinction and resuscitation of arts, and the revolutions of the intellectual world."—*Rasselas*, Chap. 30.

All this must be lost, if we be determined to blot out from the world every vestige of ancient science, and monument of ancient learning.

But the practical and great use of studying the Eastern languages is to communicate with, and to instruct the inhabitants of the East. It is not what we find, but what we are to transfuse into these languages that is valuable, and it may be regarded as axiomatical in Native education that *European knowledge cannot be extensively diffused among the natives of the East, unless it be translated into, and taught in their native tongues, and that their vernacular dialects cannot be understood thoroughly, nor used with propriety, without a knowledge of their learned languages.* That instances may be given of a few particularly clever individuals, such as the late lamented Rammohun Roy, who, with good opportunities, have acquired a considerable, or even very perfect knowledge of English, and used it as a means of acquiring information, is not to be denied; but such rare exceptions take away nothing from the truth of the general rule.

I shall make little reply to what is hinted of my aspirations after European reputation and a Professor's chair. Neither of these objects would be dishonourable if I had them in view, but it is not usual, I believe, now-a-days, to support a literary discussion, by the imputation of what are supposed to be improper motives to an opponent. Such imputations are, no doubt, always easy, but experience proves that little is gained by this mode of argumentation. Upon this head, however, it is, if necessary, easy to clear myself: a twelvemonth ago, undoubtedly I did cherish the idea that after an absence of twenty-five years I might return to my native country, and then make what honest efforts were in my power to remain. Recent events have effectually cut off this prospect, and there is little likelihood that I shall ever have the power of interrupting the canvas of any candidate for the chairs to which Mr. Trevelyan alludes.

It is not easy to understand the sense in which Mr. Trevelyan so repeatedly asserts that Persian is a dead language in India. If that be a dead language the words of which are in every one's mouth, and in which a vast proportion of literary composition, periodical publication, and epistolary correspondence is carried on, and which almost all ranks above the very lowest speak and understand, then, no doubt, Persian may be ranked as such, but on no other terms. I will venture to say that for one Native letter written in the Rekhtu, which we call Hindostanee, there are at least fifty written in Persian, containing a large proportion of Arabic.*

According to Mr. Trevelyan's views, English and Hindostanee are "to go on together till they meet in a common language." Without enquiring too curiously what is meant by two languages going on together, the result is supposed to be that a new language is to be formed out of English, Bengalee, Hindee, &c., in the same manner as English itself was formed out of the various European dialects, or Spanish out of Latin, Gothic and Arabic. I do not say that in the various combinations of mundane affairs such an event is not possible, but it appears to me nearly as improbable as any can well be. Admitting, however, that it actually does take place, still little advantage will be gained unless the whole inhabitants of the British empire can be pre-

* One can scarcely suppose the Editors of Native newspapers so blind to their own interest as to publish in a dead unintelligible language; yet all the Mohammadan newspapers are invariably in Persian, mixed with a very large quantity of Arabic. What would be thought of a project at home for publishing a newspaper in Latin or Greek? yet this is what the Native Editors, by Mr. Trevelyan's account and to use his expression, are besotted enough to do here. To accumulate authorities in proof of the common use of Persian by the inhabitants of India, is in fact, like accumulating them to prove that they commonly use rice for their food or cotton for their clothes. I may, however, mention just one more. The pupils of the Native Medical Institution,—persons certainly of no very high education,—keep a case book of the symptoms and treatment of the sick on the establishment. The language of this is left entirely to their own choice, and they uniformly write in Persian.

vailed on to unlearn their present language, and to learn Hindostanee in exactly the same proportion as Hindostanees learn English. Without this the languages must still remain distinct, and the speakers unintelligible to each other. The transposition even of thousands, perhaps tens of thousands of words, from one language to another, is not enough to render it intelligible. Thousands of words are common to French and Italian, to English and German, yet a Frenchman will not understand an Italian, nor an Englishman a German; and by Mr. Trevelyan's account, Arabic and Persian are unintelligible in Hindostan, though tens of thousands of their words are used in the common language.

This result, however, Mr. Trevelyan allows is not to take place "till after successive generations." What are we to do in the mean time? Are we to sit idle till perhaps after Herschel shall have performed some centuries of revolutions this amalgamation of languages actually takes place. Miss Martineau furnishes an answer in her last publication—"Nature is slow in her workings; and since the life of man is short, his business is to work with her, not to wait for her."—*Home's abroad.*

So it is here; we are not to wait for new languages that may possibly spring up,—it is our business to make use of those at present existing.

I shall not undertake to defend the licentiousness of Sanscrit literature, except to observe that it is a fault unfortunately common to it with the literature of many other nations, which it is rather a violent remedy to propose curing by absolutely abolishing the Sanscrit language. These are not the measures by which morality is to be advanced: it is not the destruction of Sanscrit literature, but the eradication of impure affections at which we ought to aim, and as long as these are suffered to exist, there will never be wanting immoral books in all languages. Upon Mr. Trevelyan's principle, French should be strictly prohibited, as that language contains abundance of immoral books. The plan of getting rid of Sanscrit immorality by the destruction of the whole of Sanscrit literature and language, is like that said to be practised in the

Papal dominions for the extermination of robbers: when they are suspected to be residents in a town, they are not themselves sought out for punishment, but orders are given for the destruction of the whole town altogether.

I now come to the statements made respecting my translations: it is true that I have translated into Arabic Hooper's Anatomist's Vade Mecum; that I have also translated his Physician's Vade Mecum; that I have also translated Crocker's Land Surveying, (though this was not a work of my choosing, but that of the Committee); and it is also true that I have translated the half of the first volume of Hutton's Course of Mathematics, and would have translated the whole had I been allowed. All this is true, and I am proud to think that it has been in my power, under Providence, to execute works, certainly not dishonourable to myself, and so useful to the Oriental world, and to enrich their languages with such a valuable fund of knowledge. Committees may alter, Governments change, and Colleges decay—but a well translated book, when once given to the world, can never lose its value or cease to be useful.

My remuneration, however, has by no means been 400 Rs. a month: from this is to be deducted the expence of Mouluvees, (which were always the best in my power to procure) copyists, writers, books, paper, and numerous et cæteras, the minimum of all which was 150 Rs. a month, leaving me never more than 250, and this cannot be called a very exorbitant sum for a labour which they only can judge of who have tried it, and by which I nearly ruined my health at first commencing.

If it be asked why no more Oordhoo or Bengalee translations have been made—the answer is short: because no adequate measures have been taken for the purpose. No European can undertake to translate without incurring a monthly expence of from 100 to 150 Rs. for Native assistants: if he calculates on less, he only deceives himself and deceives his employers. It is not natural to suppose that any one would make this outlay without some prospect of remuneration. Where this does not exist the business has been left chiefly, if not entirely, to Natives, who look for remuneration to the printing of their own works at their own presses, and the sale of a certain number of copies to the Committees connected with Native education. How translations thus undertaken have been executed has been explained in the letters of 𝕿. which need not therefore be repeated here. No one, I believe, has ever praised, except those who have not read them.

The labourer is worthy of his hire. Good translations, like every thing else that is good, to be had, must be paid for. He who pretends to undertake gratuitously a task that requires so much previous study, so many qualifications, and so much labour, acts like the Sircar who professes himself willing to serve Master without wages, purely for the honour of doing so. This kind of service is too well known to be infinitely the dearest of all. To have good translations, the Committee should make up their minds as to the books which they require, the languages in which they want them made, and the remuneration they are willing to give. They should then ascertain that the person who undertakes the work has a sufficient knowledge first, of the science which forms the subject of the book; secondly, of the language which he is to translate into; thirdly, of the principles of translation and the art of adapting English books to Oriental readers; and lastly, they should require from him a moderate specimen of the manner in which he is to execute the work. This should be examined by a qualified Committee, who should be requested to give their opinion unbiassedly after *an actual perusal* of the specimen and comparison of it with the original, it being understood that they are to have full liberty of speech, and that the opinions of the individual members are to be confidential and *not liable to be published to the world without their consent*. These restrictions would no doubt diminish the quantity of Bengalee and Oordhoo translations with which the Calcutta presses now groan, but most assuredly they would greatly improve the quality.

As my notions respecting the principles on which an Oriental Dictionary should be compiled, are (as Mr. Trevelyan justly remarks) identical with those of 𝕿.* it would be needless to repeat them here, and I shall make no farther observation on Mr. Thompson's book except that, without the least wish to derogate from its merits, I cannot think it (as Mr. Trevelyan seems to do) sufficient for the use of the Natives. In my opinion the labour of a whole life of the profoundest study would scarcely suffice and might be well employed in such an undertaking; and I shall assert, even at the risk of the imputation of whatever motives my readers may choose, that no measure could be more creditable to Government nor more useful in itself, than the employment of a body of well qualified men in the compilation of such a work.† To expect a private individual to undertake this is quite absurd: he would ruin his fortune and health before getting through the first letter.

I may here notice a publication of this kind that does indeed deserve commendation, that is the Murathee and English Dictionary by Captain Molesworth, and Lieutenants T. and G. Candy, lately published at Bombay. A perusal of the 16th and 17th pages of its preface will give some idea of the labour which these gentlemen have gone through so successfully and so meritoriously.

To conclude this long discussion; a good translation of the circle of the sciences into Arabic and Sanscrit would be a boon of

---

* This T is not *German*, as Mr. Trevelyan supposes, but black letter, or *Old English*. There is not, probably, a real German T in any of the Calcutta printing presses, and I am not therefore able to exhibit the difference; but there are still some books extant printed in the barbarous hieroglyphics of that language, and if Mr. Trevelyan will take the trouble of looking into any of them, he will see the true figure of a German T.

† I need not on this occasion mention the National Dictionaries compiled in Italy, France, and Spain, as instances in which Governments have not thought works of this kind unworthy of their notice. Barbarous as we may think the Chinese to be, and perhaps as they are, it is certain they have shewn themselves no barbarians in this respect, having long been in possession of the Imperial Dictionary of their language, of which, as a national work, it appears from the accounts of it, they may justly be proud. In all probability the great Arabic Dictionary of the Qaumoon was compiled under the auspices of the well known Timoor or his rival Bajazêt. The Indian Government would not be disgraced by imitating these Barbarians.

inestimable value to the Oriental world, and till we have accomplished it, all our other efforts in Native education will be maimed and imperfect; with whatever honour, to use Mr. Trevelyan's expression, the name of Lord William Bentinck may descend to posterity, I shall venture to assert that these honours would suffer no diminution, were it recorded that his administration had presented the Natives with the key to the unbounded treasury of knowledge in the shape of this compilation, and widened the intercourse between the Eastern and Western world by the formation of a scientific system of the philology of their respective languages.

I am,

SIR,

Your obedient servant,

JOHN TYTLER,

Member of the Committee of the School Book Society, for the examination of works in the Mohammadan languages.

P. S. Since writing the above I have seen in your paper of the 8th instant, Mr. Trevelyan's observations on Mr. Prinsep's second minute. It may be as well to make a few remarks on these, to avoid having to write on the subject again.

One of the first of Mr. Trevelyan's observations is, that " we have to construct a literature for Upper India from the beginning." This matter I confess appears to me in a different light. It is not our business to *construct* a literature, but *to assist and encourage the natives to construct one for themselves,*—and this can only be done by the cultivation of their own language. A National literature made by foreigners in a foreign language is a contradiction in terms; English, I admit, ought to be an object, nay, even a paramount object in Native education, but a National literature they must construct for themselves in their own languages.

I think Mr. Trevelyan should make farther enquiries before speaking contemptuously either of the medicine of Hippocrates or the logic of Aristotle. If he does, he will perhaps find that the medicine of Hippocrates is a very different thing from that with which he seems to confound it,—the physiological theories of Galen. However low we may value the latter, the former will lose its value among medical men only when the human constitution shall cease to be what it is. The Madrasah would have little to fear from its critics could they accuse it of nothing worse than the study of the medicine of Hippocrates. I shall not pretend to be very profoundly versed in Aristotle's logic, but suspect Mr. Trevelyan has not distinguished between the art of sylogistic reasoning as invented by that philosopher, and the useless subtleties added to it by his commentators. Had he done so, he might perhaps have agreed in the opinion expressed by Fielding's Dr. Harrison, "that Aristotle was not so great a blockhead as many persons think who have never read him."

Mr. Trevelyan informs us that the Delhi College youths cannot learn *two foreign languages*;* and therefore of the two, he recommends English instead of Persian. I have already examined in what sense Persian can be called a foreign language in India, and shall therefore add only, that even supposing (though by no means allowing) that Persian is foreign, still Mr. Trevelyan's conclusion cannot be allowed without the most violent strain upon the meaning of that word. Strictly speaking, French and Chinese are both foreign languages in England, but can it be maintained that they are both equally foreign and equally difficult to acquire, and that an English school boy will find it equally easy to master either? A little trial would shew that while a few months study will make him a very respectable French scholar, the labour of half his life might be hardly sufficient to gain even a moderate acquaintance with Chinese. So it is with Persian and English

---

* This is no very high compliment to the Delhi College, and it would have perhaps been better had Mr. Trevelyan (to use an expressive Scotch phrase) "keepit his thoomb upon it." Boys at a common school at home learn Latin, Greek, and French, and they find no difficulty in adding to those, when required, Italian or German. Both French and Italian are, as a matter of course, learnt by every young girl of tolerable education. Nay, however shocking Mr. Trevelyan may think it, I have heard of some young ladies actually learning Latin besides, and helping their younger brothers to make their quotas of hex and pentameters.

here: a twelvemonth will be enough to enable a native to gain a very serviceable knowledge of the former,—eight or ten years will give but a broken and imperfect acquaintance with the latter. The one already composes three-fourths of their vernacular tongue, and its idioms and trains of metaphor are those to which they are accustomed; the other has not the slightest association with any of their ideas.

I cannot see any mistake in Mr. Prinsep supposing "that Persian is essential to the business of the lives of the rising generation." Admitting the case to be as Mr. Trevelyan states, that "the only reason why English does not at once take the place of Persian in the Courts of Justice and other officers of Government is because a sufficient number of persons qualified in the English language are not at present procurable," (though this be evidently a petitio principii), still it is certain that Courts of Justice and Government Officers are by no means the greatest, and by no means the most important part of human affairs. Hundreds of thousands and millions pass their lives very happily without any intercourse with either. Could the mass of private correspondence and private transactions be collected, the records of Government and of Courts of Justice, voluminous as they may appear, would shrink before it into insignificance. All this among the Mohammadans and a large proportion among the Hindoos is carried on in Persian, without a knowledge of which a Native at all above the lowest ranks must be quite helpless. Limited as my transactions are, I yet could manage to furnish Mr. Trevelyan with a large drawer full of letlers and *arzees* on all sorts of subjects, of not more than three years old, written in Persian *by choice* from persons who know that I am equally ready to receive them whatever may be their language or character. There may be two or three Hindoostanee pieces in the collection, but so few as not to be worth mentioning, and even these are so full of Persian words and phrases, that the difference between the two languages is more nominal than real.

As to the word *Nugur*, there is no doubt that it *might* be written and pronounced in all the ways Mr. Trevelyan points out, just as our village *might* be written vallage, villuge, vollige, vulloge, and a dozen others. The only abatement is, that in Oriental characters it never *is* written or pronounced in any way but one, and that no Native will hesitate for a moment in giving to it one invariable pronunciation, whereas its Roman representative actually *is* subject to all the capricious variations of spelling and pronunciation which Mr. Prinsep represents.

Of the general run of the Bengalee translations which issue in such numbers from the Calcutta press, I have given my opinion in two or three places, and need not repeat it here. I shall therefore only say that I think they should be *read* before they are printed; or if this be too hard a condition, at any rate before they are *praised.*

In spite of all that is written and said on the subject, it is lamentable to find the public in general still so ignorant of the real state of Native education. A writer in the *Literary Gazette* of February 15th, 1834, in describing the want of adequate editors to Oriental books, seriously informs us that, " the Hindoo College is rapidly bringing forward scholars who will unite a critical knowledge of their own language to a very considerable skill in those of Europe." Had the writer of this article inquired, he would have found that the scholars of the Hindoo College learn no Sanscrit, and are unable even to read its alphabet. So far from having a critical skill in Bengalee, they declare they know nothing of its grammar, and don't understand the language so well as English. It is not very likely, therefore, they will ever give the important assistance to philologists, which the writer of the article appears to think they will be able to do.

The other parts of Mr. Trevelyan's minute have been answered in the course of the present long letter. I shall therefore here take leave of the discussion, and trust he will pardon me for doing so, in a line and a half of a dead, barbarous, and unintelligible language :—

εχθρον δε μοι εστιν
Αυτις αριζηλως ειρημενα μυθολογευειν.

ON THE POSSIBILITY, THE PRACTICABILITY, AND THE EXPEDIENCY OF SUBSTITUTING THE ROMAN IN PLACE OF THE INDIAN ALPHABET.

(Extracted from the CALCUTTA CHRISTIAN OBSERVER *for April,* 1834.*)*

The discussion respecting the substitution of the Roman in place of the Indian Alphabets has recently been revived, in consequence of the publication of Mr. Trevelyan's Minute on the proceedings of Education Committees in Calcutta. Mr. Trevelyan advocated the substitution: Dr. Tytler opposed it. The Minute of the former is the exposure and appeal of a sweeping reformer and ardent philanthropist: the rejoinder of the latter, with the exception of a few awkward attempts at sarcasm, is the production of a sober minded gentleman and accomplished scholar.

It is not my present intention to follow the remarks of either of these. Long before the recent discussion arose, the subject in dispute was forcibly brought home to my own mind, in connection with various plans for the amelioration of the people of India. And the result of my own inquiries was a decided conviction in favour of the views that have been so ably propounded by Mr. Trevelyan.

The subject I conceive to be one of far greater importance, in the *present* stage of native improvement, than most people are willing to admit, or rather than those who have not made it an object of study, are capable of comprehending. On this account, I should rejoice to see the whole question traced in all its bearings—to see it agitated in the public press, and presented in every possible form to the public mind. With the view of adding my mite to the general cause. I shall now furnish a few facts, and offer a few cursory observations.

I. *Is the proposed substitution possible?*

One party replies, yes: and another, no. Those who answer in the negative dwell chiefly on the circumstance that, in the Oriental languages, there are *peculiar* sounds, i. e. sounds *unlike* any which occur in the languages of the West. How then, ask they triumphantly, *can* these sounds be represented by Roman characters? Now, it must be owned that if these characters were of the nature of pictorial delineations, like the Mexican paintings now to be found in the Bodleian library; or of the nature of expressive symbols, similar to the Egyptian hieroglyphics; or of the nature of verbal representations, like the encyclopædic letters of China; —it would not be easy to divert them into *new* channels. But the case appears totally different when we find that alphabetical characters, like the Roman, are merely *arbitrary or conventional signs of sounds,* i. e. any character, bearing as it does, no resemblance to the sound itself, may become the sign of any sound. All that is required is, that there be a mutual understanding amongst those that employ a letter of any figure, as to the sound which such letter is intended to represent.

Since then all letters are, or ought to be, the arbitrary signs of certain *elementary sounds,* and since, in *all* languages, the *greater part* of the elementary sounds are the *same*—it follows that the *greater part* of the alphabetic letters of any language may be *directly* represented by Roman characters. Next, as to *peculiar* sounds, it may often be found, as in the Indian languages, that they are not *radically diverse* from all that find a place in the languages of the West. That which is said to be *peculiar* in the former, may be only *some particular modification of an elemental sound that* enters essentially into the latter. The difference, instead of being a radical one, may be only a difference in the tone, time, or mode of enunciating the same elementary sound. In this case, the Roman character, with some mark, above or below it, would, if agreed on by mutual consent, sufficiently distinguish the peculiarity.

This was the deliberate opinion of Sir William Jones; and as his authority ought to weigh much with even the profoundest orientalists, I shall here quote his words. "*By the help,* says he, "*of the diacritical marks used by the French, with a few of those adopted in our own treatises on fluxions, we may apply our present alphabet so happily to the notations of all Asiatic languages, as to equal the Deva Nagari itself in precision and clearness; and so regularly, that any one, who knew the original letters, might rapidly and unerringly transpose into them all the proper names, appellatives, or cited passages, occurring in tracts of Asiatic literature."*

So positive and unhesitating an opinion, delivered by such a man, may be reckoned decisive of this part of the subject. But if any lingering doubt still remain as to the possibility of representing all *peculiar* sounds by means of Roman letters with diacritical marks, there is still the expedient of effecting this end by *particular combinations of letters.* Without reverting to the excessive simplification of Wachter, who maintains that *ten* distinct characters would suffice to express all the elementary sounds that belong to the human organs; or to the more moderate opinion of Harris, who declares that "to about *twenty* plain elementary sounds we owe that variety of articulate voices which have been sufficient to explain the sentiments of such an innumerable multitude of all the past and present generations of men;" let us adopt what some would reckon the still more reasonable conclusion of Bishop Wilkins, that 34 separate characters would be requisite for the purpose, and what follows? That the Roman alphabet, being both defective and redundant, could never be made to express the sounds *not peculiar* to it? No such thing. Let any one consult the Bishop's alphabetic table, and if not satisfied with the extension of Roman letters with diacritical marks to denote *all* peculiar sounds, he cannot fail to be convinced that the object can be fully and satisfactorily accomplished, by an appropriate combination of two of the existing letters.

It is a mere fallacy to talk of the inadequacy of simple Roman letters to express *certain peculiar* sounds. No one has said that, barely and nakedly by themselves, unaccompanied by any mark or uncompounded, they can. What has been alleged is that the majority of Indian letters can be represented *directly* by corresponding Roman characters, and that the remainder can be *ade-*

quately represented by Roman characters with diacritical marks, or Roman characters suitably combined.

And after what has now been advanced may I not fairly conclude that *such* representation is in all respects *possible?*

II. Admitting the *possibility* of substituting Roman characters, under certain prescribed conditions, in place of all the Indian letters, the next question is, can such substitution be held to be *practicable?*

Those who regard it as *impracticable*, generally ask in a tone of defiance, Has such a thing ever been done—has such a thing been known or heard of?

Now, I may surely assert that, though we could not appeal to a single example in the history of the past, this would be a sorry argument. While I hold the maxim to be a sound one, that "what man *has* done, man *may* do again,"—I must hold it to be at once unsound and injurious to lay down the principle that "what man *has not* done, man *cannot* do." And yet this is the principle, on which in the present instance much of the opposition, on the score of impracticability, rests. The argument put in plain terms amounts to this: 1st, "No people ever employed the characters of a foreign language to express the ordinary and extraordinary sounds of their own: *therefore*, the attempt to accomplish this is not practicable:" 2d, "No people ever substituted the appropriate characters of another language in place of those peculiar to their own: *therefore*, the attempt to accomplish this is not practicable." This is palpably very bad reasoning, since if allowed to be valid, it would lay an arrest on all possible improvement. Applied to the inventor of the steam engine, it would stand thus: "No people ever made use of steam, as an impulsive force; *therefore* the attempt to do so, is not practicable." And so of every other invention in art, and every discovery in science. In all these cases, and in all alike, would not the proper course of procedure be; "Is the thing in itself possible? is it, as to its object, desirable? If so, let us make it practicable."

But we have conceded too much to our opponents. Past history is *not* wholly a blank in respect of examples. And as *facts* seem to weigh with them more than arguments, or abstract possibility and desirableness, I shall indulge them with a few statements of facts.

First. As to the employment of letters of one language to express the peculiar sounds of another.

The language of the Tongan Islands has various peculiar sounds; and yet these have been successfully represented, by a judicious application of the Roman letters.

The old Celtic, or Gaelic language, which is nearly the same as the old Irish, and is still spoken universally in the Highlands of Scotland, has several *peculiar* sounds, i. e. sounds to which there are none perfectly similar either in the English, or in any other of the European languages,—and yet, these sounds have been successfully expressed by Roman letters. No diacritical marks have been used. Only 18 of the Roman letters have been selected and by a skilful employment of these, not only the common, but all the *peculiar,* sounds in the language have been represented in a way that is perfectly intelligible to every Highlander.

Ought not these facts to demolish the bugbear of impracticability on this head?

Second. As to the national substitution of one set of characters in place of another widely dissimilar in form.

In Europe, these substitutions have been notoriously frequent from the earliest ages.

Before the conquest of Gaul by Cæsar, the old Gaulish letters, which somewhat resembled the Gothic, were alone used in that country. After the subjection of the Gauls to the Roman yoke, the letters of the conquerors, though extremely dissimilar, were universally introduced, and substituted in place of their own. Towards the close of the 6th century the Roman Gallic letters were again changed by the Francs, into what was called the Franco-Gallic, or Merovingian. This was succeeded, a few centuries afterwards, by the German mode of writing, which had been improved by Charlemagne. In the 12th and 13th century, the modern Gothic, the most diversified, complicated, and barbarous of all alphabets, supplanted the German letters. And at the time of the Reformation, the Roman once more usurped the place of the existing alphabet, and has ever since maintained its ground.

In England the changes were not less numerous. At one time the German mode of writing prevailed; at another, the Saxon; at another, the modern Gothic, &c. and finally, the Roman.

In different parts of Ireland and Scotland, similar dialects of the old Celtic language have been spoken for at least 18 centuries. There were peculiar letters, of a form distinct from that of other alphabets, to express all the elementary sounds of this ancient language. These letters have been used chiefly by the Irish Celts, are commonly known under the designation of the "old Irish character." Now, when, about a century ago, great efforts began to be made to improve the condition of the Scottish Celts, the alphabet that contained appropriate letters to express the ordinary and peculiar sounds of their language, was set aside, and the Roman notation of letters universally adopted. And in that character have all works ever since, without one single exception, been printed.

Whether the practice be as yet uniform, I cannot tell, but I have also seen translations of the Bible and the confession of faith into the Irish dialect, published in the Roman character.

In Spain, during the earliest period of its history, letters were used, somewhat similar to the Greek. After the Romans became lords paramount of the soil, they introduced the general use of their own letters. When the country was overrun by the Visigoths, they abolished the Roman and substituted their own very different form of writing. In the 11th century, by the decree of a Synod held at Leon, the alphabet of the Visigoths was superseded by the restoration of the Roman characters.

In Italy, from the vicissitude of its fortunes, the mode of writing was often changed. At one time, the Lombardic mode of writing entirely set aside the use of the Roman letters, being adopted even in the Bulls of the Popes: at another, the modern Gothic, &c.

Though in most of these cases, the forms of the letters were as widely different as can well be imagined, it may still be objected, however absurdly, that they all belong to the languages of the West. Of the people of the East, their languages, manners, customs, &c. unchangeableness has been predicated!

In removing even this cavil, the following *facts* may be of some service:

Who more tenacious of every thing Jewish, than the descendants of Abraham? And yet it is generally allowed that the old Hebrew character, now known under the name of the Samaritan, was abandoned during the time of the Babylonish captivity, and that the Chaldaic form, which is vastly different, was substituted in its place, and has been ever since retained.

Originally the Arabic alphabet, as asserted in the learned Dr. Hales' Analysis of Chronology, was the same as the Syriac, which differs as much from the modern Arabic alphabet, as it does from the Chaldaic and old Hebrew. This total change in the order and form of the Arabic letters took place about the commencement of the Mohammedan æra.

The old Persian or Zend, which is said by Jones to approach to perfection, was superseded by the Arabic alphabet, which has been adopted by all nations that have embraced the religion of Mohammed.

But, what some may think still more to the purpose, has not the Persian character been often practically employed in representing Indian words, particularly in the Upper and Western Provinces? And, *vice versa,* has not the Nagari character been employed in expressing Persian and Arabic terms? The Oordoo, which is a compound of Persian and Indian words, has been represented indifferently by Persian or Nagari letters. And if so, why not this, and other Eastern languages by the Roman?*

---

* I have been told by a friend, who has derived his information *direct* from M. Alexander Csoma de Körös, the celebrated Hungarian, who has thrown so much

Rather, if so many and such radical substitutions of one form of letters, for another totally dissimilar, have actually taken place in the West, and in the East, does not the voice of history loudly and emphatically protest against the baseless notion, that to substitute the Roman, in place of the Indian letters, is impracticable? Does not the testimony of experience, as it rolls along different ages and different countries of the world, perfectly demonstrate that such substitution is, and must be pronounced to be, in every point of view *practicable?*

III. On the supposition of the possibility and practicability of the proposed change, is it *expedient* to substitute the Roman, in place of the Indian letters?

Those who oppose the expediency of the substitution often argue thus: "Look at the English orthography; Jones himself pronounces it to be disgracefully, and almost ridiculously imperfect: Look, on the other hand, at the Indian orthography; its precision, clearness, and regularity cannot well be surpassed:—would it not then be most inexpedient to disturb the beauteous order of the latter by introducing the irregularities of the former? and this sort of reasoning is backed by what some account a few good jokes and pithy sarcasms at the expense of our poor English orthography.

---

light on the language and literature of Thibet, that the *general structure* of the Hungarian language is so *very unlike* the parent stock of any of the dialects of the west, and so *exactly like* the Sanscrit, that he doubts not the Hungarian and Sanscrit are essentially connected as to their *original source,* if not, as Primitive and Derivative. And this conclusion, deduced from the striking *similarity of structure,* is greatly confirmed by the equally striking *similarity* in the *names* of the *most common objects.* M. Körös is of opinion, that the Huns had undoubtedly an original alphabetic character of their own when they first invaded Europe, and that it was retained by them till their conversion to Christianity, when *they adopted the Roman character.*

If this be the case, and the peculiar philological attainments of M. K. render his opinion worthy of the highest possible respect, what a remarkable *corroboration* does it afford of all that has now been advanced? A language possessing originally a peculiar alphabetic character of its own—and what is more, *a language radically Indian in its structure and terms—has for ages been successfully represented by Roman characters?*

But it will not do to pass off this subject by mere orthographical jokes and sarcasms. There is a radical fallacy in the reasoning of these gentlemen. They suppose that we really wish to introduce the absurd anomalies of English orthography into the East, and without this supposition, their argument is good for nothing. Now this *supposition* is a *most barefaced assumption. It cannot be conceded, because it is not true.* We do *not* wish to see the anomalies of *English* orthography incorporated with the languages of the East. Neither do we wish to see superfluous Roman characters employed. If, in the East, one alphabetic letter uniformly represents one elementary sound, *let the Roman letter substituted in its place be invariably appropriated to the expression of that sound.* This is what we propose : and, in this way, I should like to know where a corner can be found for a single anomaly—or how the greatest possible clearness, precision, and regularity may not be attained? In this view of the case, the potent arguments of our learned Orientalists must fall with deadly effect on *their own false premises.*

If then the reasons usually urged *against* the expediency of the substitution be utterly *groundless,* let us now state a few reasons *in favour* of it.

1. The substitution is expedient, because thereby we should obtain an alphabet more perfect than any of our Eastern alphabets—more perfect even than the Deva Nagari.

This may startle the idolizers of Sanscrit; but nevertheless, it can be proved to be true. What are the requisites of a perfect alphabet? Without specifying the whole I may remark that, by the common consent of the soundest philologists, the following are of the number:—As every separate elementary sound ought to have a separate character to express it, so none but separate elementary sounds ought to have separate characters. Elementary sounds, radically the same, but differing somewhat in the tone, time, or mode of enunciation, ought not to have representative characters wholly different in form.

Now, in *both* these respects, the Deva Nagari is exceedingly imperfect.

Consonant sounds, such as the two *ds* and the two *ts* marked by Jones *d* and *d'*, *t* and *t'*, though radically the same, and differing in the *tone* of pronunciation, are represented by characters totally different.

Vowel sounds, such as the long and short *a*, the long and short *i*, &c. which of course differ only in the *time* of their pronunciation, are expressed by separate characters.

Sounds *not* elementary, i. e. compound sounds, which ought surely to be expressed by a combination of the elemental or simple sounds that compose them, are represented by separate letters. Of this description are *all* the *aspirated letters*, which form so large a proportion of the Deva Nagari and other Indian alphabets. Who can say that this is not a very *unnecessary multiplication* of alphabetic characters? How vastly more rational and philosophical the simple expedient of having *one* clear *mark*, or *letter*, for the aspiration, which could be applied to *all* vowels and *all* consonants. This is the expedient, not less admirable in theory than convenient in practice, which has been resorted to in the European alphabets. And if, after this truly philosophical model, the Sanscrit and other Indian alphabets were framed anew, we should at once get rid of a great number of very *superfluous* characters.

2. It follows from this that the proposed substitution is expedient, because, by rendering the Indian alphabets more perfect, and thereby getting quit of *many wholly useless letters*, the *complexity* which at present characterizes these alphabets would be greatly diminished, and the *progress* of *every learner* in the *same degree* facilitated.

3. The substitution is expedient, as it would remove one grand impediment to the free reciprocation of sentiment and feeling among the millions of Hindoostan.

To illustrate this, let me revert to an example. If a book in Latin, English, French, Spanish and Italian were presented even to an unlearned Englishman, in the Roman character, he would readily perceive that numberless words, and roots of words, were the *same* in all; and would conclude that the study of one, two, or more of these might be a comparatively easy task, in consequence of this *palpable radical similarity*. But were the book presented in Roman, Modern Gothic, Old Gaulish Visigothic, and Lombardic characters, he could scarcely be persuaded that under forms so wholly different there could lurk any similarity at all. And the study would be regarded a forbidding, difficult, if not, a hopeless one. So actually stands the case in India; the number of *dialects* is immense: and each dialect must have letters of a different figure. Let then a specimen of each be presented to an unlearned Hindoo: what must be his conclusion?—What *can* it be, except that his country abounds with totally *different languages?* And if so, the attempt to hold any communication with natives not of his own province, must be abandoned as hopeless. Now were the whole presented, in *the same character*, it would be *seen* and *felt* that the natives are not divided into so many sections of foreigners to each other—that they have *all fundamentally* the *same* language—and that without much difficulty a community of interest and a beneficial reciprocation of thought might be effected to an extent at present unknown, and from the repulsive aspect of so many written characters, deemed utterly impracticable.

4. It is expedient, as it would tend mightily to encourage the study of the English language.

In the present state of things this is a matter of paramount importance. Of all earthly boons, the bestowment on a native of a sound English education, is beyond all question the highest and the noblest. It is by the quickening impulse of the knowledge to be derived through the medium of English that we are to expect the *first* awakening of the national mind from its present lethargy. Now by the universal introduction of Roman characters, every Hindoo might become familiar with them from infancy. The study of English would no longer be looked upon as *entirely new*, nor the language *entirely foreign*. It would appear in all respects more inviting: yea, it would allure thousands to engage in it who are now scared away altogether from the task.

5. It is expedient, as regards the enriching of the Indian languages.

If there must be an infusion of a vast number of *new ideas* into the languages of the East, ere the dense *mass* of the people can be elevated in the scale of moral and intellectual being, there must be a corresponding number of *new terms* to express these. Now, while it is conceded that the Indian letters are well suited to the expression of Indian sounds and words, every Orientalist must bear me testimony in saying, that they are *very ill adapted* to the expression of sounds and words in foreign languages. By the adoption, therefore, of Roman characters, the incorporation of *new terms*, implying an accession of *new ideas*, may go on indefinitely, without any difficulty, and without any confusion.

6. The substitution is expedient, as it would save much valuable time and useless trouble to hundreds, and thousands, and tens of thousands of our fellow-creatures.

It cannot be doubted that soon great numbers in every province from the Himalaya to Cape Comorin, will be engaged in the study of English. These, of course, *must* become acquainted with the Roman character. Besides, it will always be the lot of many to study more than one of the Indian dialects. What a prodigious saving of time and trouble must it then be, to multitudes in every province of Hindoostan, to be possessed of *one common alphabet?* Our *great* Orientalists, our Philological giants, I know, will convert this into a subject for derision or scorn, because *they* can master a new alphabet in a week :—but I cannot help it. In spite of *their* thundering *canons,* I must be allowed to assert, without fear of contradiction, that the *majority* of mankind cannot in the course of a week, acquire the *same facility* and *speed* in *reading* and *writing* a totally *new* set of alphabetic characters as they enjoy in reading and writing those with which they have been long familiar. No : *such* acquisition is *generally* the result not of five or six days' practice, but of at least as many months. Why, then, *waste* so much precious time upon *nothing?* He who, in acquiring *new* languages or dialects, would *voluntarily* choose a *new* set of letters for each, instead of adopting one already known, appears to me to act the part of the foolish traveller who, on reaching every *new* river, instead of availing himself of the established ferry-boat that awaited his arrival, would prefer lingering on the banks in order to construct a *new* one for himself, in which to cross to the other side.

7. The substitution is expedient, as thereby a prodigious amount of expense will be saved to the community.

It is a fact, that, from the intricacy—the complexity of most of the Indian characters, it is utterly impossible to reduce them to so small a size as the Roman may be, without rendering them altogether indistinct, or even illegible. In this way, twice the quantity of typal matter, twice the quantity of paper, and nearly twice the quantity of binding materials and labour, must be lavished for nought. Now, considering that we have to provide books for a hundred millions of people, this surely is a consideration of too grave and important a nature to be overlooked.

On the whole, I conclude from principle and not from prejudice, in favour of Mr. Trevelyan's scheme. And not until the preceding facts are proved to be untrue, and the inferences unsound, shall I cease to advocate the possibility, the practicability, and the expediency of substituting the Roman instead of the Indian Alphabets.

ALPHA.

P. S. To render this paper complete, a representation of the Nagari and Persian alphabets, (the two principal ones used in India) in Roman characters may be given in the next number of the Observer.

A SCHEME FOR REPRESENTING THE DE'VA NA'GARI' AND PERSIAN ALPHABETS IN ROMAN CHARACTERS.

(Extracted from the CALCUTTA CHRISTIAN OBSERVER *for May,* 1834.*)*

It has been already shewn,* in a *general way*, that the substitution of the Roman in place of the Indian Alphabets, is as *possible* and *practicable*, as it is unquestionably *expedient*. And it now remains to ascertain and exemplify the *particular mode* in which the substitution may be best effected.

This is the more necessary at the *present* time, since different methods have been proposed by different men eminent for their talents, and profound as oriental scholars—and since inextricable confusion must ensue, unless those who advocate the contemplated change, agree as to some fixed and uniform system of notation.

Whoever wishes for information relative to the earlier attempts by Davy, Williams and Halhed, to express Indian in Roman characters, is referred to the first volume of the Asiatic Researches. In the same volume is an elaborate account of the system adopted by the celebrated Sir William Jones. The labours of Dr. Gilchrist in this field are very generally known. Foster, Carey, Shakespear, Haughton, and others have also lent their aid in solving the problem that regards the *best practical method* of adapting the Roman to the Oriental alphabets—a problem for the most successful solution of which a premium has been held out by the Asiatic Society of Paris.

All of those now named have adopted and applied, with more or less success, certain prosodial, accentual, or algebraic symbols. Recently, however, Messrs. Arnot and Forbes, in several valuable elementary treatises, published in London, have suggested the adoption of "a system of writing like the Hindee-Persi-Arabic,

---

* See Page 66: No. IV. of the Calcutta Christian Observer: the Courier of 2nd April: the Hurkaru and India Gazette of 3rd April: and the Englishman of the 4th and 5th April.

to which several Oriental nations have partly contributed, by calling in the aid of two or three of the European alphabets most generally known." Hence, an Italian letter, a Spanish letter, a Persian letter, and Greek letters have been intermixed with Roman letters. This may possibly be the readiest way of conveying to self-taught Europeans some idea of the *sound* of each letter; but assuredly it is not the most comely to the sight, nor the most suitable in practice.

On the whole, after the maturest consideration of the subject, it appears beyond all dispute, that Sir William Jones' system, with such alterations and modifications as experience has suggested, is not only the simplest in itself, but the most convenient in practice, as well as the most susceptible of *universal* application. And it carries with it one special recommendation, that it is already familiar to every Oriental scholar, in every part of the known world. It is therefore proposed to adopt and apply this system, altered and modified, to a certain extent, to all Alphabets whether of Sanskṛit or Persian origin.

These being the two chief sources of all the Indian alphabets, it is expedient primarily to represent them. For these being once successfully represented, all the rest will easily follow; since no other Indian Alphabet contains sounds radically dissimilar. And the few anomalies that do occur, will best be explained under each of the alphabets that are only so many branches springing from the two parent stocks.

I. The letters of the Roman alphabet, which may be successfully employed for the representation of the Sanskṛit and Persian alphabets, are the following:—a, b, d, e, f, g, h, i, j, k, l, m, n, o, p, q, r, s, t, u, v, w, y, z. But these, even when used singly, are employed so irregularly in English orthoëpy, that it is absolutely necessary at the outset to fix the precise sound which in the proposed scheme they are intended *invariably* to express.

Short Vowels.

a, has uniformly one sound, and that is the shut or short a; or ă, as represented by lexicographers. It occurs in such words as *America, adept, quota,* &c., and must never be confounded with the sound of a, in *mate, fate ; fall, all ; far, tar,* &c.

i, the short or shut sound, as in *fit, sit, pin,* &c.—never as in *fine, mite, pine,* &c.

u, the short obtuse sound—as in *bull, pull*—never short, as in *but, rut,* &c.—nor long, as in *mute, pure, secure,* &c.

Simple Consonants.

b, has its regular sound, as in *bed, bell,* &c.

d, has the soft dental sound formed with the point of the tongue, slightly pressed on the roots of the upper teeth, nearly as in *duke, due ;* or still more nearly, as the soft French dental *d* in *des,* &c.

f, has its regular sound, as in *fit, fix,* &c.

g, has its regular hard sound, as in *got, go,* &c. Never soft, as in *gender, gentle,* &c.

h, has its regular sound, as in *house, horse,* &c. It is the letter that expresses the aspiration of any other.

j, has its regular sound, as in *jam, join,* &c.

k, has its regular sound, as in *keep, king,* &c.

l, has its regular sound, as in *law, land,* &c.

m, has its regular sound, as in *man, mind,* &c.

n, has its regular sound, as in *nap, nay,* &c. It is the nasal that corresponds with the dental letters.

p, has its regular sound, as in *pot, pan,* &c.

q, has nearly the same sound, as in *quack, clique, quoit,* &c. It has been happily described by Gilchrist as " our *k* articulated by raising the root of the tongue simply towards the throat, which must not be in the smallest degree ruffled. The *q* may consequently be styled a deep, but liquid lingual letter, produced by clinking the root of the tongue against the throat, so as to cause a sort of nausea. The same sound will be recognized when pouring water in a particular manner from a long-necked goglet, as the liquid decanting may represent the lower part of the tongue acting upon the throat or neck of the vessel in question, unruffled by the water gushing from it."

r, has its soft sound, as in *morn, scorn,* &c.

s, has its regular sound, as in *sin, dusk,* &c.

t, has the soft dental sound, formed with the point of the tongue, slightly pressed on the upper front teeth, nearly as in *tube, tunic,* &c. It resembles, says Dr. Carey, the Yorkshire pronunciation of *t* in *butter*. It also resembles as nearly as possible the soft French dental *t* in *tu,* &c.

v, has its regular sound, as in *vain, vale,* &c.

w, has its regular sound, as in *way, wet,* &c.

y, has its regular sound, as in *yea, yes,* &c.

z, has its regular sound, as in *zeal, zone,* &c.

The greater part of the foregoing letters may be employed *directly*, with the sounds now explained *invariably* annexed to them, to represent corresponding letters in the Sanskṛit and Persian alphabets, thus:

Rom.	a	i	u	b	d	f	g	h	j	k	l
Sans.	अ	इ	उ	ब	द		ग	ह	ज	क	ल
Pers.	ا	اِ	اُ	ب	د	ف	گ	ه	ج	ک	ل

Rom.	m	n	p	q	r	s	t	w	v	y	z
Sans.	म	न	प		र	स	त		व	य	
Pers.	م	ن	پ	ق	ر	س	ت	و	و	ي	ز

In this clear, distinct, and satisfactory manner, can all those letters that are of *most frequent* occurrence be *directly* expressed by Roman letters, unmarked by accents or points, and uncompounded.

II. We come now to a class of letters, the sounds of which not being *radically* diverse from the fundamental sounds already expressed, may be accurately represented by certain appropriate marks. In these the difference exists chiefly either in the elongation of the short vowel sounds, or in a varied pronunciation of consonant sounds. And for the sake of distinction and uniformity, it is proposed to distinguish *elongated* sounds by *accents* placed above,* and *varied* sounds, by *dots* placed underneath.

Long Vowels.

á, with an accent, has *invariably* the long broad sound, as in *father, ask*, &c.

e, has *invariably* the long broad sound, nearly as in *there*, or as *ei* in *neighbour*, or exactly as *e* in the French *tempête, flèche*, &c.

í, with an accent, *invariably* as long slender *i*, in *police*, or as *ee* in *feel, sleep*, &c.

o, *invariably* long, as in *note, cold*, &c.

ú, with an accent, *invariably* the long obtuse sound, as in *rude, rule*, &c.

Consonants with diacritic marks.

ḍ, with a dot below, is the hard palatial *d*, formed by forcibly striking the tongue against the palate or roof of the mouth; nearly like *d* in *dull, ladder*, &c. The English *d* may be said to be somewhat softer than this Indian *d*, and somewhat harder than the Indian dental *d*. It, however, more nearly resembles the former than the latter. Still, as the latter occurs *ten times* more frequently than the former, it is deemed advisable to restrict the *dot* to the former; on the principle that it is expedient to employ diacritic marks as little as possible.

ḥ, with a dot below, is the common *h*, sounded more forcibly in the throat, nearly as in *hay, hot*, &c.

ṇ n̤ ṇ̤, with *one, two*, or *three* dots below, are nasals corresponding respectively to the three classes of linguals, palatines, and gutturals. The latter two are not often used, unless compounded with another letter: and as that letter determines the class

* In the case of *e* and *o*, which have not, like *a, i*, and *u*, any corresponding short sound among the short vowels, the accent over the letter is unnecessary, and is therefore omitted.

of the n, the dots may in such case be omitted. The reason there are so many nasals is thus distinctly explained by Haughton, "In the Déva Nágarí alphabet no change takes place in sound without a corresponding change in writing; in consequence, as the sound of the nasals entirely depends upon the consonant, by which it is followed, it will, for this reason, depend upon the latter, what form the nasal shall assume in writing. As an example, the sound of *n* in *king* is different from the sound of *n* in *lent*, (and from the sound of *n* in *launch*,) and for the first the guttural ṉ would be required, and for the last the lingual ṇ, (and for the other the palatine ṉ,) if it were desired to represent these words in Déva Nágarí characters; because the *g* of *king* is guttural, and the *t* of *lent*, lingual," (and the *ch* of *launch*, palatine.) Hence ṇ is sounded with the point of the tongue reverted to the palate, as *n* in *lent*: ṉ, "by pressing the whole breadth of the tongue into the hollow of the palate, the tip turned downwards, and by forcing the sound through the nose, with the mouth open something like *gn* in the French *digne*:" ṉ like the French *n* in *sans, bon*; or like *ng* in *ring, sing*, &c.

ṣ ṣ, with *one* or *two* dots below, lik *s* in *see, sin*, &c. These are only introduced to distinguish two Persian letters, the sounds of which, as used by the people of India, are in reality identical with that of the common *s*, i. e. possess the same phonic value.

ṭ, with a dot, stands exactly in the same relation to *t*, as ḍ does to *d*. It is uttered by striking the point of the tongue on the palate, nearly as in *tub, tin*, &c.

ṭ, with two dots, and a slight shade of difference in the sound, is the Persian *toé*, so marked to correspond with *zoé* of the same class of letters.

ẓ ẓ ẓ, with *one, two* or *three* dots below, are all of them sounded by the people of India, like *z* in *zeal, zone*, &c.. They are here adopted merely to distinguish three Persian letters that differ in form, but not in sound.

The following, then, are the letters that may be clearly represented by Roman characters, with diacritical marks.

Rom.	á	e	í	o	ú	ḍ	ḥ	ṇ	ṇ̤	ṇ̬	ṣ	ṣ̤	ṭ	ṯ	ẓ	ẓ̤	ẓ̬
Sans.	आ	ए	ई	ओ	ऊ	ड		ण	ञ	ङ			ट				
Pers.*	ء	آي	ي	و	و		ح				ص	ث	ط		ض	ظ	ذ

ạ, with a dot below, may represent the singular vowel-consonant ع named *ígn*, as in *sign*. "It is," says Shakespear, "one of the guttural letters, being formed in the lower part of the throat. Its sound has been compared to the voice of a calf calling its mother, or to that of a person making some painful exertion." "This letter," says Mr. Yates in his valuable Hindústaní Grammar, "is generally pronounced *a* or *i*, sometimes long and sometimes short." When short, it may fitly be expressed by ạ, ị. When long by ạ́, ị́, agreeably to the notation already explained. To mark the distinction of these vowels from the others, a dot is placed below them.

III. We next proceed to describe those letters, chiefly *compound*, that may most satisfactorily be represented by a *combination* of two or more Roman characters.

Anomalous Vowels and Diphthongs.

ṛi, with a dot under it, to distinguish it from the consonant *r*, is reckoned a vowel in Sanskṛit, and is pronounced, as in *r*ill, *r*ich, &c.

ṛí, is the same sound elongated, as in ma*rine*, or *ree* in *ree*d.

lṛi, is nothing but ṛi with the liquid l placed before it, and pronounced simultaneously.

lṛí, is ṛí, with the liquid l similarly placed before it.

ai, which is compounded of a and i, and is pronounced like *ai* in *ai*sle, *oi* in *oi*l, or *ie* in d*ie*, &c.—but a little broader.

au, which is compounded of a and u, and is pronounced like *ou* in *ou*r, *ow* in *ow*l, &c.—but a little broader.

---

* The mode of using these will be explained more fully afterwards.

To these are commonly added °, or *ang*, a very strong nasal, as in *gang:* and :, or *ah*, a silent *h*, generally employed as a final.

Compound Consonants.

There is a class of consonants which many have accounted simple sounds, for the expression of which there is no *single* letter in the Roman alphabet. But these have been, and may be, *adequately* represented by an appropriate *combination* of letters.

These letters are *c, g, k, s, z*, followed by *h*—not the strong aspirating *h*, but *h* soft and subservient, i. e. *h* so modifying the sounds of *c, g, k, s, z*, as to aid in producing the peculiar sound required, thus:

ch, is sounded *invariably* like *ch* in cheat, church, China, &c.

g̣h, or Persian g̣h-ígn, with a dot below it, to distinguish it from the aspirated Sanskṛit *g*, soon to be noticed. It is a peculiar guttural sound, like the Northumberland *r*, or that sound which is heard when gargling the throat with water.

ḳh, or Persian ḳhe, with a dot below it, to distinguish it from the aspirated Sanskṛit *k*. It is a guttural sound like the Greek χ as pronounced by the Scotch; or *ch* in the Scotch word *loch;* or *ch* in the German *macht*. "It is," says Gilchrist, "the rough guttural *k*, pronounced in the very act of hawking up phlegm from the throat."

sh, is sounded exactly like *sh* in *shine, shell*, &c.

ṣh, with a dot below it, is pronounced in the same way as *sh;* and is so marked, because it has a distinct letter in Sanskṛit, and as a sibilant, belongs to the class of linguals, which have been similarly marked.

zh, is sounded exactly like *z* in *azure, s* in *pleasure*, or the French *j* in *jour*.

There is another class of consonants compounded of single letters and the aspirate, i. e. aspirated consonants. To express the aspirate, the Greeks employed a small mark like an inverted comma (ʽ). The Romans substituted *h;* and this letter is, for various reasons, the most convenient for the expression of the Indian aspirates. These, by the annexation of *h* to the single consonants, may be most significantly represented. Care must be taken, however, not to pronounce the consonants with the aspirate *as one sound,* which generally happens in the European alphabets. Each letter in the combination must have its sound audibly enunciated, though both sounds be closely united.

b'h or bh, is *b* aspirated and pronounced as in Ho*b*-*h*ouse; or, dropping the first syllable, *b*-*h*ouse.

ch'h or chh, is *ch* aspirated, as in chur*ch*-*h*ill; or, dropping the first part, *ch*-*h*ill.

ḍ'h or ḍh, is the dental *d* aspirated.

d'h or dh, is the lingual *d* aspirated, as in col*d*-*h*and, or *d*-*h*and.

g'h or gh, is the hard *g* aspirated, as in do*g*-*h*ouse, or *g*-*h*ouse.

j'h or jh, is *j* aspirated, as soft *g* in colle*g*e-*h*all, or *g*e-*h*all.

k'h or kh, is *k* aspirated, as in mil*k*-*h*ouse, or *k*-*h*ouse.

p'h or ph, is *p* aspirated, as in u*p*-*h*ill, or *p*-*h*ill.

t'h or th, is the dental *t* aspirated.

ṭ'h or ṭh, is the lingual *t* aspirated, as in fa*t*-*h*en, or *t*-*h*en.

These illustrative words are written at length, to convey, if possible, the notion of the consonant and the aspirate's being each distinctly enunciated: and they are contracted, to shew that in the enunciation of the combined letters, they must not be too much separated.

The following, therefore, are all the *combined* letters required to complete the representation of the Indian Alphabets:

Compound Vowels.

Rom.	ṛi	ṛí	lṛi	lṛí	ai	au	ang	ah
Sans.	ऋ	ॠ	ऌ	ॡ	ऐ	औ	ं	ः
Pers.					ي	و		

Peculiar Combinations.

Rom.	ch	gh	kh	sh	ṣh	zh
Sans.	च	—	—	श	ष	
Pers.	چ	غ	خ	ش	—	ژ

Aspirated Consonants.

Rom.	chh	dh	ḍh	gh	jh	kh	ph	th	ṭh
Sans.	छ	ध	ढ	घ	झ	ख	फ	थ	ठ
Pers.	—	—	—	—	—	—	—	—	—

We have now completely exhausted all the letters in Sanskṛit and Persian alphabets. In the former, the compound letter क्ष is generally added; but it is exactly represented by *ksh.* Let us then collect and arrange all the foregoing letters agreeably to the Indian mode of alphabetic order.

The De'va Na'gari' Alphabet.

Vowels.

अ a, आ or ा á; इ ि i, ई ी í; उ ु u, ऊ ू ú; ऋ ृ ṛi, ॠ ॄ ṛí; ऌ ऌ lṛi, ॡ ॡ lṛí; ए े e, ऐ ै ai; ओ ो ó, औ ौ au; ं ang, ः ah.

Consonants.

Gutturals,	क k, ख kh;	ग g, घ gh;	ङ n.
Palatines,	च ch, छ chh;	ज j झ jh;	ञ n.
Linguals,	ट ṭ, ठ ṭh;	ड ḍ, ढ ḍh;	ण ṇ or cerebrals.
Dentals,	त t, थ th;	द d, ध dh;	न n.
Labials,	प p, फ ph;	ब b, भ bh;	म m.
	य y, र r;	ल l, व v;	
	श sh, ष ṣh;	स s, ह h;	क्ष ksh.

Of the two last orders of letters, h ranks with the gutturals; y and sh with the palatines; r and ṣh with the linguals; l and s with the dentals; and v with the labials.

Persian Alphabet.

ا a, آ á, إ i, أ u.	ت t	چ ch
ب b,	ث ṣ	ح ḥ
پ p	ج j	خ kh

د	d	ط	ṭ	م	m
ذ	z̤	ظ	ẓ	ن	n
ر	r	ع	ạ, á, ị, í, &c.	و	w or v; as vowels, ú, ó, or au.
ز	z	غ	gh	ه	h
ژ	zh	ف	f	ي	y; as vowels, í, é, or ai.
س	s	ق	q		
ش	sh	ک	k		
ص	ṣ	گ	g		
ض	z̤	ل	l		

Concluding Remarks.

I. In the above scheme for Nágarí consonants, the inherent vowel or short अ has been omitted. It may however be supplied by any one in reading the alphabet thus, ka, kha—ga, gha—ṇa, &c. the *a* being the obscure short *a* in *America*, or like *a* in *adrift*. It is more agreeable to the genius of the Roman Alphabet to supply this vowel in writing or printing, instead of leaving it to be understood.

When no vowel is subjoined to a consonant, it is supposed to be quiescent. And the small mark (्) that usually indicates a silent consonant, is not subscribed, in order to preserve a uniformity between the Nágarí and Persian Alphabets.

The letter क or *k* was represented by Sir William Jones by *c*, and the letter श or *sh* by *s'*. The former has been altered as too indefinite, and the latter as not being uniform. For the sake of distinction the accentual mark (′) has been applied only to vowels and not to consonants: besides it is now universally acknowledged that *sh*, as in *ṣhort*, is the true sound.

The nasals also have been more minutely distinguished by diacritical marks.

For all languages derived from the Sanskṛit, such as the Bengalí, Hinduí, Uriya, Marathí, the above scheme may be successfully applied.

II. The greatest difficulty in the Persian Alphabet has been the representation of the different *s*, *t*, and *z*'s. The practical difficulty, however, is greater in appearance than in reality, as those letters with the diacritical marks are of unfrequent occurrence. Indeed it has been adopted as a standing rule, that these marks should be used as sparingly as possible—and when used, should be restricted to these letters that more rarely enter into the composition of words.

To prevent misconception, it may be proper to explain here somewhat more fully the Persian system of vowels.

There are three short vowels—َ zabar ;—ِ zér ;—ُ pésh : zabar and pésh being written above, and zér below, the letter which it follows in the enunciation. Thus بَ ba, بِ bi, بُ bu.

A letter having one of these accompanying it, expressed or understood, is said to be *harkat*, or movable by that vowel. Thus, in بَ ba, *b* is movable by zabar : in بِ bi, *b* is movable by zér : in بُ bu, *b* is movable by pésh. If there is no short vowel expressed or understood, the consonant is said to be *sakin* or quiescent. Thus بَر *bar*, not *bara*, *bari*, or *baru*, &c.

ا Alif, when beginning a word or syllable, is reckoned by oriental grammarians, a very slight aspirate, like *h* in *hour*. But its chief purpose is to subserve the expression of short or long vowels. Thus, اَ a, اِ i, اُ u—short vowels. Again, ا with ~ above it, generally written آ, is the long vowel á. So آ, when the last letter of a word or syllable, preceded by another letter with zabar (´) above it, (and it is always so preceded,) becomes the long vowel á, as in بَا bá, &c.

وَ Wao, when movable by a short vowel, or beginning a word or syllable, is a consonant like *w* in *with*, and sometimes as *v* in *void*. Thus, وَ wa, &c. But وْ quiescent, i. e. terminating a word or syllable, when preceded by a letter movable by zabar (ʹ) forms the diphthong *au*, like *au* as pronounced by many in *caustic*, or *ou* in *loud*. Thus بَوْ *bau*, &c. Again, وْ quiescent, preceded by a letter movable by pésh (ُ) forms the long vowel u, like *u* in *rude*, or *oo* in *moon*. Thus بُو bú, &c. This combination, however, in Persian has often the power of long ó, as *o* in *whole*, *more*, &c. Thus, بُو *may be* sounded *bó*, &c.

ي Ya, when movable by a short vowel, or beginning a word, or syllable, is a consonant like y in *yet*. Thus, يَ ya, &c. But يْ quiescent, when preceded by a letter movable by zabar (َ) forms the diphthong ai, like *ai* in *aisle*, or *i* in *fine*, &c. Thus, بَيْ *bai*, &c. Again, يْ quiescent, preceded by a letter movable by zér (ِ) forms the long vowel í, like *i* in *marine*, or *ee* in *feel*. Thus بِي *bí*, &c. But in Persian this combination has often the sound of long broad *e*, like the French ê in naivetê, &c.*

Hence it appears that in Persian there are three short and five long vowels, and two diphthongs.

Three short, as in اَ a, اِ i, اُ u : or in بَ ba, بِ bi, بُ bu.

Five long, as in آ á, or بَا bá ; بِي bí or bé ; بُو bú or bó.

Two diphthongs, as in بَيْ bai ; بَوْ bau.

---

* Whoever wishes for a simple and concise view of Persian Grammar, will find it in the admirable elementary works of Messrs. Arnot and Forbes of the London Oriental Institution.—To be had of Messrs. Thacker and Co. Calcutta.

In Roman characters three short, a, i, u : five long, á, í, é, ú, ó : two diphthongs, ai, au.

Hence in reading Romanized Persian, nothing can be easier than to reverse the process, by substituting, if required, the Persian in place of the Roman letters.

The scheme now proposed will suffice for all languages which bear a close affinity to the Persian, such as the Hebrew, Arabic, Syriac, Chaldee, Samaritan, &c.

III. It would be easy to find other Roman letters which might express the sounds of the Nágarí and Persian Alphabets. For instance *a, á* might be short *u* and *au, aw, eo, o, oa,* or *ou,* as in *taught, law, George, nor, groat, thought,* &c. Instead of *i* and *í;* we might have *i, ee, ie,* &c. Instead of *u, ú;* we might have *oo, ou, eu, ew,* &c. Instead of *é, ai;* we might have *ay, ai, i, oi,* &c. Instead of *ó, ou;* we might have *oa, ow,* &c. But it is conceived impossible for any letters to represent the sounds in question more concisely or more appropriately than those which have been adopted.

If this has been fully substantiated, (and it can readily be verified by any one who will take the trouble to ponder the subject in all its bearings,) then, for the sake of that uniformity which is so truly desirable, it is to be hoped that every one will be disposed to merge private differences in one grand general plan for the securing of national benefits:—it is to be hoped, that one and all will be cheerfully prepared to sacrifice little partialities and peculiarities of opinion at the shrine of the PUBLIC GOOD.

P. S. The author, in behalf of several others, who with himself advocate the substitution of the Roman character, embraces this opportunity to notify, that it was once their intention to make a direct personal application to Oriental scholars, generally, for their opinion, as to the best practical method to be adopted in the proposed substitutionary process. On farther consideration, however, it has been deemed most expedient, in order to save time and labour, and prevent unintentional partialities, to make this general appeal to all those literati who take an interest in the subject. Be it then understood, that if any individual has any suggestions to offer, he is hereby solicited to make known the same, through the medium of the Christian Observer, or any other public journal. Conscious only of a sincere desire to promote the welfare of the people of India, we are open to *sound advice, from whatever quarter it may proceed.* Any *real* improvement that may be pointed out, will receive speedy and due attention. *But should none be suggested which is likely to meet with general approbation, the scheme now propounded may be considered as final.*

Not to swell this paper to an inordinate length, it is proposed to insert in the next Observer a complete representation of all the principal alphabets in Eastern India; together with specimens of the different languages and dialects, in Roman characters. In conclusion, the author has here gratefully to acknowledge the valuable assistance derived, in drawing up the preceding paper, from the suggestions of the Rev. Messrs. Yates and Pearce—gentlemen whose separate and united labours in the cause of native improvement are too well known to require any statement on his part.

ALPHA.

A REPRESENTATION IN ROMAN CHARACTER OF THE PRINCIPAL ALPHABETS IN EASTERN INDIA, WITH NOTICES OF DIALECTIC PECULIARITIES, SPECIMENS OF THE MODE OF APPLYING THE LETTERS IN PRACTICE, AND ANSWERS TO OBJECTIONS.

(*Extracted from the* CALCUTTA CHRISTIAN OBSERVER *for June,* 1834.)

The scheme developed in the last Observer for representing the Deva Nágarí and Persian alphabets in Roman characters has excited a warmer interest, and secured a more general acquiescence, than could well have been anticipated. It has led in some quarters to frequent conversations and repeated discussions, and drawn forth from other various communications of a nature at once friendly and instructive. Every thing around us seems decisively to prognosticate the ultimate triumph of our designs.

When "the scheme" was put forth, observations were solicited from all whose course of study might qualify them to form a practical judgment on the subject. Nor was the solicitation fruitless. While approbation of by far the greater part has been expressed, a few, and only a very few, alterations have been proposed. These it is proper now briefly to notice. They may be divided into two classes:—those that may, and those that cannot, well be adopted.

1. The latter class, or that which includes the alterations that cannot well be adopted, refers exclusively to certain letters, which, though originally identical in sound, and though still retained in the original form, yet, in consequence of the mutations to which all things human are liable, have become, in different alphabets, somewhat changed in phonic power. To exemplify what is meant, take the first letter in every Indian alphabet, the Deva Nágarí अ or short *a*. "This," says Sir William Jones, "is the simplest element of articulation, or vocal sound. The word *America* begins and ends with it. In our own anomalous language, we commonly mark this elementary sound by our *fifth* vowel (or short *u*). The Nágarí letter is called acár; but it is pronounced in Bengal like our *fourth* vowel (or short *o*); and in the west of India like our *first*." In Hindústání, our short *u*, as in *up*, *sun*, &c. would exactly represent this letter. Hence it is so represented by Dr. Gilchrist. Our short *u* being thus pre-occupied, the Dr. was obliged to express उ and ऊ, or our short obtuse and long obtuse *u*, as in *push*, *cube*, by the symbols *oo* and oo. Now, if we had to do *only* with Hindústání, this probably might be the most appropriate notation. But our object is totally different, we have to provide for *all* the Indian alphabets. The question is not, what will suit *best one particular* alphabet; but what, so far as we can judge, will suit *every* alphabet best, so as to secure the nearest possible approximation to a *universal conformity?* How, for instance, would Dr. Gilchrist's short *u*, as in

up, answer in the Bengalí, where the letter is sounded like our short *o?* How would it suit in those dialects where it is pronounced like our *a?* Would it, in these several instances, answer the purpose better than short *a*, as in *America?* Surely not. And if not, since we have to make provision for *all* the alphabets, and forestall the peculiar deviations from the parent stock in each,—is it not better, more consistent, more uniform, to employ the letter which exactly represents the corresponding one in the *primitive* Indian alphabets, and mark as *anomalous* in any particular *dialect* the *retention* of the *original letter*, while the pronunciation is more or less *varied?* In this case, most palpable it is that the *anomaly* lies not in our system of representation, but is wholly chargeable on the varying powers of the *literal form* represented. And if it be distinctly borne in mind, that *our concern is not with what may answer best in this or that language, but with what may, on the whole, answer best in all the Indian languages, sure we are that this single circumstance of paramount importance were enough to obviate every difficulty, and remove every objection that can possibly arise on the present head.*

2. The other class, or that which embraces alterations that may well be adopted, appears to be restricted to the two vowel sounds *e* and *o*, and to the nasal *ns*.

In no Indian language are the vowels *e* and *o short.* They retain *invariably* the *long* sound. Still, as we find the *short* and *long* sound of *a*, *i*, and *u* perpetually occurring, and as it was necessary to mark this difference, it was proposed, in accordance with established usage, to let the *simple* letters express the *short* sound, and distinguish the *long* sound, by accents placed above them; thus *a*, *á*, &c. Since then an *accent* became the special symbol of an *elongated* sound, it was deemed proper, for the sake of *uniformity*, to place it over *e* and *o*, as well as over long *a*, *i*, and *u*. And it cannot for a moment be doubted that this preserves the unity and harmony of the system, by effectually excluding any thing like inconsistency or contradiction. On the other hand, it has been urged, that these letters (*e* and *o*), and especially *e*, pervade the language to a greater extent than perhaps any others —and that we ourselves laid down the indisputable canon, that "it is *expedient* to employ diacritic and other marks as sparingly as possible." Influenced by these and other reasons, we have resolved to drop the accent from the long vowels *e* and *o*—assured that no mistake can arise, when we apprize the learner that these, in every Indian language and dialect, possess *invariably* the *long* sound,—the former nearly like *e* in *there*, or exactly like *e* in the French *tempête*; and the latter like *o* in *note*.

Again, with reference to the nasal *ns*, it has been suggested, that the notation may in *practice* be simplified. Of this no doubt was ever entertained. In "the scheme" it was shewn, how by a few dots these nasals might be distinguished with the utmost precision. To save repetition, let the reader consult the explanation there given. He will find that the different classes of gutturals and palatines have each a nasal *n*, marked respectively ṇ̬, ṇ̱. Now it so happens that these are *never interchanged*, i. e. the ṇ̬, belonging to the gutturals, never precedes a palatine letter; the ṇ̱, belonging to the palatines, never precedes a guttural. In this case, the notation of *n* in practice may be perfectly intelligible without farther precision. That is, if n without any dot, be found preceding a guttural, the reader may be sure it can be none other than ṇ̬; if preceding a palatine, it can be none other than ṇ̱; and if preceding s or sh, h or a semivowel, none other than ng. By attending to this plain remark we shall get quit of several dots—and so simplify the practical use of the Roman character.

Altogether, when we consider the conflicting state of opinions on this subject amongst orientalists, we have been delightfully surprised at the average rate of unanimity that now prevails amongst those friendly to the substitution—an auspicious concord, that must proceed from the noble resolve to sacrifice selfish partialities on the altar of social well-being and national prosperity.

These preliminary remarks we shall now follow up by giving in separate tables the two parent alphabetic stocks, with the derivatives principally employed in Eastern India.

1.—*The Deva Nágarí and its branches.*

Vowels.

Bengali.	Deva Nágarí.	Kaithí Nágarí.	Mahráthi.	Uriya.	Burman.	Butan.	Sound in Roman character.
অ	अ	अ	𑘀	ଅ	အ	ཨ	*a*
আ	आ	आ	𑘁	ଆ	အာ	ཨཱ	*á*
ই	इ	इ	𑘂	ଇ	ဣ	ཨི	*i*
ঈ	ई	ई	𑘃	ଈ	ဤ	ཨཱི	*í*
উ	उ	उ	𑘄	ଉ	ဥ	ཨུ	*u*
ঊ	ऊ	ऊ	𑘅	ଊ	ဦ	ཨཱུ	*ú*
ঋ	ऋ	ऋ	𑘆	ଋ*	—	རྀ	*ṛi*
ৠ	ॠ	ॠ	𑘇	ୠ*	—	རཱྀ	*ṛí*
ঌ	ऌ	ऌ	𑘈	ଌ*	—	ལྀ	*lṛi*
ৡ	ॡ	ॡ	𑘉	—	—	ལཱྀ	*lṛí*
এ	ए	ए	𑘊	ଏ	ဧ	ཨེ	*e*
ঐ	ऐ	ऐ	𑘋	ଐ	အဲ	ཨཻ	*ai*
ও	ओ	ओ	𑘌	ଓ	ဩ	ཨོ	*o*
ঔ	औ	औ	𑘍	ଔ	ဪ	ཨཽ	*au*
ং	·	·	·	ଂ	အံ	ཨཾ	*ang*
ঃ	:	:	:	ଃ	အား	ཨཿ	*ah*

* Sounded ṛu, rú, lṛu, in the Uriya alphabet.

Bengálí.	Deva Nágarí.	Kaithí Nágarí.	Máhrathí.	Uriya.	Burman.	Butan.	Sound in Roman character.
ক	क	𑂍	𑘎	କ	က	ཀ	*k*
খ	ख	𑂎	𑘏	ଖ	ခ	ཁ	*kh*
গ	ग	𑂏	𑘐	ଗ	ဂ	ག	*g*
ঘ	घ	𑂐	𑘑	ଘ	ဃ	གྷ	*gh*
ঙ	ङ	𑂑	𑘒	ଙ	င	ང	*n*
চ	च	𑂒	𑘓	ଚ	စ	ཙ*	*ch*
ছ	छ	𑂓	𑘔	ଛ	ဆ	ཚ*	*chh*
জ	ज	𑂔	𑘕	ଜ	ဇ	ཛ*	*j*
ঝ	झ	𑂕	𑘖	ଝ	ဈ	ཛྷ	*jh*
ঞ	ञ	𑂖	𑘗	ଞ	ည	ཉ	*n*
ট	ट	𑂗	𑘘	ଟ	ဋ	ཊ	*t*
ঠ	ठ	𑂘	𑘙	ଠ	ဌ	ཋ	*th*
ড	ड	𑂙	𑘚	ଡ	ဍ	ཌ	*d*
ঢ	ढ	𑂛	𑘛	ଢ	ဎ	ཌྷ	*dh*
ণ	ण	𑂝	𑘜	ଣ	ဏ	ཎ	*ṇ*
ত	त	𑂞	𑘝	ତ	တ	ཏ	*t*
থ	थ	𑂟	𑘞	ଥ	ထ	ཐ	*th*
দ	द	𑂠	𑘟	ଦ	ဒ	ད	*d*
ধ	ध	𑂡	𑘠	ଧ	ဓ	དྷ	*dh*
ন	न	𑂢	𑘡	ନ	န	ན	*n*
প	प	𑂣	𑘢	ପ	ပ	པ	*p*
ফ	फ	𑂤	𑘣	ଫ	ဖ	ཕ	*ph*
ব	ब	𑂥	𑘤	ବ	ဗ	བ	*b*
ভ	भ	𑂦	𑘥	ଭ	ဘ	བྷ	*bh*
ম	म	𑂧	𑘦	ମ	မ	མ	*m*
য	य	𑂨	𑘧	ଯ	ယ	ཡ	*y*
র	र	𑂩	𑘨	ର	ရ	ར	*r*
ল	ल	𑂪	𑘩	ଲ	လ	ལ	*l*
ব	व	𑂫	𑘪	ବ	ဝ*	ཝ	*v*
শ	श	𑂬	𑘫	ଶ	သ*	ཤ	*sh*
ষ	ष	𑂭	𑘬	ଷ	—	ཥ	*ṣh*
স	स	𑂮	𑘭	ସ	—	ས	*s*
হ	ह	𑂯	𑘮	ହ	ဟ	ཧ	*h*
ক্ষ	क्ष	𑂍𑂹𑂭	𑘎𑘿𑘬	କ୍ଷ	ဠ*	ཀྵ	*ksh*

* The Burman and Butan letters thus marked are pronounced anomalously.

2.—*The Arabic and its branches.*

Hindustání.	Persian.	Arabic.		Hindustání.	Persian.	Arabic.	
آ اَ اِ اُ	ا	ا	a,á,i,u,	ڑه	—	—	ṛh
ب	ب	ب	b	ژ	ژ	—	zh
بھ	—	—	bh	س	س	س	s
پ	پ	—	p	ش	ش	ش	sh
پھ	—	—	ph	ص	ص	ص	ṣ
ت	ت	ت	t	ض	ض	ض	ẓ
تھ	—	—	th	ط	ط	ط	ṭ
ٹ	—	—	ṭ	ظ	ظ	ظ	ẓ
ٹھ	—	—	ṭh	ع	ع	ع	ạ á ị ụ
ث	ث	ث	ṣ	غ	غ	غ	ḥh
ج	ج	ج	j	ف	ف	ف	f
جھ	—	—	jh	ق	ق	ق	q
چ	چ	—	ch	ک	ک	ک	k
چھ	—	—	chh	کھ	—	—	kh
ح	ح	ح	ḥ	گ	گ	—	g
خ	خ	خ	ḳh	گھ	—	—	gh
د	د	د	d	ل	ل	ل	l
دھ	—	—	dh	م	م	م	m
ڈ	—	—	ḍ	ن		ن	n
ڈھ	—	—	ḍh	ں	—	—	ṉ
ذ	ذ	ذ	ẓ	و	و	و	w
ر	ر	ر	r	ه	ه	ه	h
ڑ	—	—	ṛ	ی	ی	ی	y

Note.—In the above tables, all the regular letters, with their proper sound, are given. This is in accordance with our plan of reserving explanations of particular variations or anomalies for each of the alphabets separately. But ere we proceed farther, it may be interesting and useful to collect and arrange in one tabular view all the Roman characters, combinations, &c. with such points and marks as have been adopted to complete the representation of the Indian Alphabets.

Out of all the Alphabets arises the following complete Roman Alphabet.

Letter.	Name.	Sound.
a	akár, as in	*A*meric*a*.
á	ákár, as in	*a*rt.
ạ ạ́ &c.	aign, as in	*jama*.
ai	aikár, as in	*ai*sle.
au	aukár, as ow	in co*w*.
ang	anuswár, as in	s*ung*.
ah	visarga,	*ah*.
b	ba, as in	*b*ut.
bh	bha, —	ho*b*-*h*ouse.
ch	cha, —	*ch*ur*ch*.
chh	chha, —	chur*ch*-*h*ill.
d	da, —	*d*uke.
dh	dha, —	ma*d*-*h*ouse.
ḍ	ḍa, —	ba*d* col*d*.
ḍh	ḍha, —	col*d*-*h*and.
e	ekár, —	there.
f	fa, —	*f*it.
g	ga, —	*g*ot.
gh	gha, —	do*g*-*h*ouse.
g̣h	g̣ha, —	*gh*astly.
h	ha, —	*h*ave.
ḥ	ḥa, —	*h*ouse.
i	ikár, —	*i*n.
í	íkar, —	pol*i*ce.
j	ja, —	*j*am.
jh	jha, —	colle*ge*-*h*all.
k	ka, —	*k*eep.
kh	kha, —	mil*k*-*h*ouse.
ḳh	ḳha, —	lo*ch*, (Scotch.)
ksha	ksha, —	bri*ck*-*s*hop.
l	la, —	*l*and.
lṛi	lṛikár, —	ful*l*-*r*ill.

Letter.	Name.		Sound.
lṛí	lríkar,	as in	ful*l*-*ree*l.
m	ma,	—	*m*an.
n	na,	—	*n*ap.
ṇ	ṇa,	—	*n*ot.
ṉ	ṉa,	—	bo*n*, (French.)
o	okar,	—	n*o*te.
p	pa,	—	*p*an.
ph	pha,	—	u*p*-*h*ill.
q	qa,	—	cli*qu*e.
r	ra,	—	*r*ace.
ṟ	ṟa,	—	ete*r*nel, (French.)
ṟh	ṟha,	—	Boe*rh*aave, (Greek.)
ṛi	ṛikar,	—	*ri*p.
ṛí	ṛíkar,	—	*ree*l.
s	sa,	—	*s*in.
ṣ	ṣa,	—	*s*ahib.
s̤	s̤a,	—	hi*ss*.
sh	sha,	—	*sh*all.
ṣh	ṣha,	—	*sh*ot.
t	ta,	—	po*t*.
th	tha,	—	po*t*-*h*ouse.
ṭ	ṭa,	—	fa*t*.
ṭh	ṭha,	—	fa*t*-*h*en.
u	ukar,	—	p*u*sh.
ú	úkar,	—	c*u*be.
v	va,	—	*v*ain.
w	wa,	—	*w*et.
y	ya,	—	*y*our.
z	za,	—	*z*eal.
ẓ	ẓa,	—	——
z̤	z̤a,	—	*z*one.
z̤̣	z̤̣a,	—	*z*ephyr.
zh	zha,	—	a*z*ure.

It has been already stated, that in the derivative alphabets, certain anomalies, such as the *retention* of the *original* letter, with a *different pronunciation*, &c. have in the lapse of time slowly crept* in. This circumstance alone were sufficient to ex-

---

* We cannot in connection with this subject refrain from quoting a few extracts from the truly admirable grammar of the Gælic language, by the late Rev. Dr. Alexander Stewart: "In the first exhibition," says he, "of the sounds of a living language, by alphabetical characters, it is probable that the principle which regulated the system of orthography was, that every elementary sound should be represented by a corresponding character, either simple or compounded; and that the same sound should be represented by the same character. If different sounds were represented by the same letter;—if the same sound were represented by different letters;—if more letters were employed than were necessary to exhibit the sound;—or if any sound were not represented by a corresponding character; then the written language would not be an adequate representation of the spoken. It is hardly to be supposed that in the first rude attempt at alphabetical writing, the principle above laid down could be strictly and uniformly followed. And though it had, yet, in the course of a few generations, many causes would occur to bring about considerable departures from it. A gradual refinement of ear, and increasing attention to euphonia; contractions and elisions brought into vogue by the carelessness, or the rapidity of colloquial speech, or by the practice of popular speakers; above all, the mixture of the speech of different nations, would introduce numberless varieties into the pronunciation. Still those who wrote the language might choose to adhere to the original orthography, for the sake of retaining the radical parts, and preserving the etymon of vocables undisguised; and for maintaining an uniformity in the mechanism of the inflections. Hence the pronunciation and the orthography would disagree in many instances, till at length it would be found expedient to alter the orthography, and to adapt it to such changes in the speech or spoken language, as long use had established; in order to maintain what was most necessary of all, a due correspondence between the mode of speaking and the mode of writing the same language.

"It will probably be found on inquiry, that in all languages, when the speech has undergone material and striking changes, the written language also has varied in a considerable degree, in conformity to these changes; but that it has not scrupulously kept pace with the spoken language in every smaller variation. The written language of the Greeks suffered many changes between the time that the old Pelasgic was spoken and the days of Demosthenes. The various modes of pronunciation, used in the different districts of Greece, are marked by a diversity in the orthography of the written language. The writing of the Latin underwent considerable alterations between the era of the Decemviri and the Augustan age; corresponding, no doubt, to the changes which had taken place during that interval, in speaking the Latin. English and French books printed within the last cen-

pose the emptiness of the boast, that absolute *regularity* and *unchangeableness* characterize the Indian alphabets. But our object is not to recriminate: our wish is merely to point out the actual state of things, in order to facilitate the progress of the learner. With this view, we shall endeavour to mark what may be termed the *anomalies* or *peculiarities* of some of those dialects which, from their proximity to us, require *immediate* attention; it is chiefly the discrepancies found to exist between certain letters and their modern phonic power. There are two ways of marking these anomalies. Thus in Bengalí the Deva Nágarí व or *v* is retained and written ব or *v*. But, the natives almost without exception now pronounce it not *va* but *ba*, exactly the same as ব or *ba*, from which also it is not to be discriminated in shape. *Either* then we must represent this letter always by *v*, and place some mark above or below it, to denote that the current pronunciation is not *v* but *b*; *or*, we must at once represent it by *b*, the actual modern sound, and place some mark above or below it, to signify that it is the *anomalous b*, or the *b*, which exactly expresses the *modern* sound of the ancient *v*. On the whole, the latter seems to be the preferable expedient. Let us then in imitation of many learned orientalists adopt the horizontal (–), and let us define it to be the symbol that denotes *anomalies* or *peculiarities* in particular dia-

---

tury exhibit a mode of orthography very different from what is found in books printed two or three hundred years ago. These instances show the tendency which the written language has to follow the lead of the spoken language, and to maintain a certain degree of conformity to those modes of pronunciation, which are from time to time adopted by those who speak it.

"On the other hand, numberless examples might be adduced from any living language, to prove that the written language does not adapt itself, on all occasions, and with strict uniformity, to the sounds of speech. Words are written differently which are pronounced alike. The same combination of letters, in different situations, represent different sounds. Letters are retained in writing, serving to point out the derivations of words, after they have been entirely dropped in speaking.

"From such facts as these, it appears a just conclusion, that written language generally follows the spoken language through its various revolutions, but still at a certain distance; not dropping so far behind as to lose sight of its precursor, nor following so close as to be led through all its fantastic deviations.

lects. Thus, if in Bengalí we meet with the word "b̲eba" in Roman character, we shall at once conclude that this is not the regular *b,* but the anomalous *b,* that expresses the current sound of the ancient *v,* and so with other letters.

With this explanation, we shall proceed to delineate, as proposed, the existing anomalies in those dialects in which books are to be *immediately* prepared.

1.—*Anomalies in Bengálí.*

The letters ড *da* and ঢ *dha* are very frequently pronounced *ra* and *rha,* with the tip of the tongue reverted to the palate. To mark this deviation in Bengálí, a point is usually placed beneath the letters; thus ঢ় *rha.* Now let us retain *r,* which expresses the *sound,* and distinguish it as *anomalous* by the horizontal (–), and thus we shall obtain *r̲a* and *r̲ha.* Whenever, then, we meet with *r̲a* or *r̲ha,* we shall know that these exhibit the *anomalous* sound of ড *da* and ঢ *dha.*

The letter য *ya* is often pronounced *ja*; and when য retains its genuine sound *ya,* it is distinguished by a dot put below it, as য় *ya.* To express its *anomalous* sound *ja,* let us adopt our fixed symbol, and write *j̲a.*

The letter ব *va,* when used *anomalously* for *b,* will be written *b̲a.*

The letter ব *va,* when following a consonant, with which it is combined, has the sound of *wa:* thus in দ্বারা, through or by, ব is subjoined to দ, and the word pronounced *dwárá.* Hence, ব used anomalously for *w,* is marked *w̲.*

জ্ঞ *jna* compounded of জ *ja* and ঞ *na,* the palatine nasal, sounded like *gn* in the French *digne.* It is however pronounced *gya* with a nasal sound. জ্ঞ therefore will be represented by *g̲y̲a.*

ক্ষ *ksha* is ক *ka* and ষ *sha,* but is always sounded *khya.* It will therefore be represented by *k̲h̲y̲a.*

ঁ, named Chandra-bindu, properly speaking, is the common *n,* but in Bengálí is used as a symbol often written over vowels, to express a strong nasal sound, like *n* in the French *bon,* or *ng* in *ring*, as in বাঁশ, which is pronounced *báṉs*, a bamboo. We must therefore represent it by *aṉ*. In Hindustání, it is written as a component part of the word.

Table of Anomalies.

Letters.	Proper sound.	Anomalous sound.
ড	ḍa	*ṟa*
ঢ	ḍha	*ṟha*
ব	va	*ḇa*
—	—	*w̱a*
জ্ঞ	jṉa	*g̱y̱a*
ক্ষ	ksha	*ḵẖy̱a*
ং	aṉ	*aṉ*

The first letter অ a is generally corrupted by the people of Bengal into an obscure sound like *short o,* in *dot, cot,* &c. This must be remembered by all who read the Bengálí Romanized.

2. *Anomalies in Hindúí.*

The ड *ḍ* and ढ *ḍha* are often pronounced *ra* and *rha,* as in Bengálí, by reverting the tip of the tongue to the palate. ड and ढ, therefore, are represented by *ṟa* and *rha.*

ष *sha* is commonly sounded as *kha.* It is, in this case, expressed by *ḵha*.

क्ष *ksha* is sounded like *chha,* and is expressed by *c̱ẖha.*

Table of Anomalies.

Letters.	Proper sound.	Anomalous sound.
ड	ḍa	*ṟa*
ढ	ḍha	*ṟha*
ष	sḫa	*ḵha*
क्ष	ksha	*c̱ẖha*

3. *Anomalies in Hindustání, &c.*

The letters ڈ *ḍa* and ڈھ *ḍha* are often sounded *ṟa* and *ṟha,* and must be expressed as before, *ṟa, ṟha.*

N

Anomalous sounds of various letters in the other languages might here be pointed out, such as ث which in Arabic is often sounded *th*, &c. :—with more important variations in Butan, Burman, &c.:—but we purposely omit them at present, because not *immediately* required, and because it is our intention to prefix to every book that may be prepared in any language or dialect, a table of regular and anomalous sounds in the alphabet of the particular language or dialect;—which tabular representation may form the key to the easy and infallible decyphering of the contents of the work. And the specimens now given in Bengálí, Hinduí, and Hindustání may serve as illustrations of the facility with which not only ordinary but extraordinary sounds may be represented in Roman character.

Having thus unfolded the common and anomalous sounds in the three Indian alphabets that more *immediately* concern us, we now present a few specimens in the Romanized form :—

BENGA'LI'.

PARABLE OF THE PRODIGAL SON.

In Bengálí character.

Luke xv. 11—24.

১১ এক ব্যক্তির দুই পুত্র ছিল; তাহার কনিষ্ঠ পুত্র পি
১২ তাকে কহিল, হে পিতঃ, তোমার বিষয়ের যে অংশ
১৩ পাইব তাহা বিভাগ করিয়া দেও। তাহাতে পিতা নিজ
সম্পত্তি ভাগ করিয়া তাহাকে দিলে পর সেই পুত্র সমস্ত ধন
একত্র লইয়া দূর দেশে প্রস্থান করিয়া দুষ্টাচরণেতে সমস্ত
১৪ সংস্থান উড়াইয়া দিল। পরে সে দেশে মহা দুর্ভিক্ষ
উপস্থিত হইল, এবং তাহার সকল ধন ব্যয় হইলে তাহার
১৫ দৈন্য দশা ঘটিতে লাগিল। পরে তদ্দেশীয় এক গৃহস্থের
আশ্রিত হইলে, সেই ব্যক্তি শূকরপাল চরাইতে তাহাকে
১৬ পাঠাইয়া দিত; কিন্তু তাহাকে কেহ কিছু আহার না দেও
য়াতে সে শূকরের খাদ্য খোশাপ্রভৃতিদ্বারা উদর পূর্ণ করিতে

১৭ বাঞ্ছা করিত। অবশেষে সে মনে২ চেতনা পাইয়া কহিল,
হায় আমার পিতার নিকটে কত২ বেতনগ্রাহিদাস যথেষ্ট
১৮ আহার পাইতেছে, কিন্তু আমি ক্ষুধায় মরিতেছি। অতএব
এখন উঠিয়া পিতার নিকটে গিয়া এই কথা বলিব, হে
পিতঃ, ঈশ্বরের বিরুদ্ধে এবং তোমার নিকটে পাপ করি
য়াছি, একারণ তোমার পুত্র বলিয়া বিখ্যাত হইবার যোগ্য
১৯ নহি; আমাকে আপনার এক বেতনগ্রাহি দাস করিয়া
২০ রাখুন। ইহা ভাবিয়া সে গাত্রোত্থান করিয়া পিতার নি
কটে গমন করিল; তাহাতে তাহার পিতা দূরহইতে তা
হাকে দেখিয়া ধাবমান হইয়া তাহার গলা ধরিয়া তাহাকে
২১ চুম্বন করিল। তখন পুত্র তাহাকে কহিল, হে পিতঃ
ঈশ্বরের বিরুদ্ধে এবং তোমার নিকটে পাপ করিয়াছি,
অতএব এখন তোমার পুত্র বলিয়া বিখ্যাত হইবার যোগ্য
২২ নহি। কিন্তু তাহার পিতা নিজদাসদিগকে আজ্ঞা দিয়া
কহিল, সর্ব্বোত্তম বস্ত্র আনিয়া ইহাকে পরাও, এবং ইহার
অঙ্গুলীতে অঙ্গুরীয় দেও, এবং ইহার পায়েতে পাদুকা
২৩ দেও, আর হৃষ্ট পুষ্ট বাছুর আনিয়া মার, তাহা ভোজন
২৪ করিয়া আমরা আনন্দ করি। যে হেতুক এই যে আমার
পুত্র সে মৃত হইয়া এখন সজীব হইয়াছে, ইহাকে হারা
ইয়া পুনশ্চ পাইয়াছি; তাহাতে তাহারা আনন্দ করিতে
লাগিল।

The above, in Roman character.

11 Ek byaktir dui putra chhila ;

12 Táhár kanishṭha putra pitáke kahila, He pitah, tomár bishayer je anshá páiba táhá bibhág kariyá deo.

13 Táháte pitá nij sampatti bhág kariyá táháke dile par, sei putra samasta dhan ekatra laiyá dúr deshe prasthán kariyá dushṭácharaṇete samasta sansthán uṟáiyá dila.

14 Pare se deshe mahá durbhikhya upasthit haila, ebang táhár sakal dhan byay haile táhár dainya dashá ghaṭite lágila.

15 Pare taddeshhíya ek grihashṭer áshrita haile, sei byakti shúkar-pál charáite táhake maṭhe paṭháiyá dila ;

16 Kintu táháke keha kichhu áhár na deoyáte se shúkarer khádya khoshá prabhriti dw̱árá udar púrṇa karite bánchá karita.

17 Abashesẖe se mane mane chetaná páiyá kahila, Háy ámár
pitár nikate kata kata betangráhi dás jatheshṭa áhár páiteche,
kintu ámi kẖudháy maritechhi.
18 Ata-eb ekhan uṭhiyá pitár nikate giyá ei kathá baliba, He pi-
tah, I'shwarer ḇiruddhe ebang tomar nikate páp kariyáchi, e
káran tomár putra baliyá ḇikhyáta haibár jogya nahi.
19 A'máke ápnár ek betangráhi dás kariyá rákhun.
20 Ihá bhábiyá se gátrotthán kariyá pitár nikate gaman karila;
táháte táhár pitá dúrhaite táháke dekhiyá dhábamán haiyá
táhár galá dhariyá táháke chumban karila.
21 Takhan putra táháke kahila, He pitah, I'shwarer ḇiruddhe
ebang tomár nikate pap kariyáchhi, ata-eb ekhan tomár pu-
tra baliyá ḇikhyáta haibár jogya nahi.
22 Kintu táhár pitá nij dásdigke ágyá diyá kahila, Sarbottam
bastra ániyá iháke paráo, ebang ihár angulete anguríya deo,
ebang ihár páyete páduká deo.
23 Ar hṛishṭa pushṭa báchhur ániyá mára, táhá bhojan kariyá
ámrá ánanda kari.
24 Je hetuk ei je ámár putra se mṛita haiyá ekhan sajíb haiyá-
che, iháke háráiyá punaschha páiyáchhi; táháte táhárá ánan-
da karite lágila.

HINDUI'.

PARABLE OF THE PRODIGAL SON.

In Nágarí character.

Luke xv. 11—24.

११ किसी मनुष्यके दो पुत्र थे। उनमेंसे छुटकेने पितासेकहा
कि हे पिता संपत्तिमेंसे जो मेरा भाग होवे दीजिये तब
१२ उसने उन्हें उपजीवन बांट दिया। और बक़ुत दिनबीतने
पाये छुटका पुत्र सबकुछ एकठा करके परदेशको चखनि
१३ कला और वहां कुकर्म्ममें अपनी समस्त संपत्ति नष्ट
१४ किई। और जब वुह सबकुछ उठाचुका उस देशमें बडा

१५ अकाल पडा और वुह दरिद्र होने लगा। तब वुह जाके
उस देशकी एक प्रजाका सेवक बना और उसने उसे अपने
१६ खेतोंमें भेजा कि सूअरोंको चरावे। और वुह लालसा
राखता था कि उन छिलकोंसे जो सूअर खाते थे अपना
१७ पेट भरे और कोई उसे न देता था। और जब वुह
अपने चेतमें आया उसने कहा कि मेरे पिताके कितने
बनिहार हैं जिनकी रोटी बचरहती है और मैं भुखसे
१८ मरताहों। मै उठोंगा और अपने पिता पास जाऊंगा
और उसे कहोंगा किहे पिता मैं स्वर्गके और तेरे आगे
१९ अपराधी हों। और अब मैं योग्य नही कि तेरा-पुत्र
कहाओं मुझे अपने बनिहारोंमेंसे एकके समान बनाइये।
२० तब वुह उठके अपने पिता पास आया परंतु जब वुह दूर
हीथा उसके पिताने उसको देखा और दयाल हुआ
और दौडा और उसके गलेमें गिरके उसे चुमने लगा।
२१ और पुत्रने उसको कहा कि हे पिता मैंने स्वर्गका और
तेरा अपराध किया है और अब इस योग्य नही कि
२२ तेरा पुत्र कहाओं। तब पिताने अपने सेवकोंको कहा
कि अच्छेसे अच्छे बस्त्र लाओ और इसको पहिनाओ और
२३ उसके हाथमें अंगुठी और पाओंमें जूती पहिनाओ। और
वुह मोटा बछडा इधर लाओ और मारो कि हम खावें
२४ और आनंद करें। क्योंकि मेरा यह पुत्र मर गया था
और फेर जीता है वुह खोगया था और मिल गया है
तब वे आनंद करने लगे।

The above, in Roman character.

11 Kisí manukhyake do putra the ;

12 Un-men-se chhutkene pitáse kahá, ki he pitá, sampatti-men-se jo merá bhág howe, díjiye ; tab usne unhen upajívan bant diyá.

13 Aur bahut din na bítne paye, chhutká putra sab kuchh ekathá karke, pardeshko chal niklá, aur wahán kukarmamen apní samasta sampatti nashta kií.

14 Aur jab wuh sab kuchh uṭhá chuká, us deshmen̲ bar̲á akál
pará; aur wuh daridra hone lagá.
15 Tab wah jáke, us desh ké ek prajáká sebak baná; aur usne
use apne kheton̲ men̲ bhejá ke súron̲ ko charáwe.
16 Aur wuh lálasá rakhtá thá ki un chhilkonse jo súr kháte the
apná pet bhare; aur koí use na detá thá.
17 Aur jab wuh upne chetmen̲ áyá, usne kahá, ke mere pitáke
kitne baníhár hain̲ jinkí roṭi bach rahtí hai, aur main̲ bhúkhse
martá hon̲.
18 Main̲ uṭhon̲ga aur apné pitá pás jáúnga, aur use kahonga, ki
he pitá, main̲ sw̲argake aur tere áge aparádhí hon̲.
19 Aur ab main̲ jogya nahí ki terá putra kaháon; mujhe apne
baniharon̲ men̲-se ek ke samán banáiye.
20 Tab wuh uṭh ke upne pitá pás áyá; porantu jab wuh dúrhí
thá, uske pitáne usko dekhá, aur dayál huạ, aur daur̲á, aur
uske galemen̲ girke, use chumne lagá.
21 Aur putra ne usko kahá, ki he pitá, main̲ ne sw̲urgaká aur
terá aparádh kiyá hai, aur ab is jogya nahín̲ ki terá putra
kaháon̲.
22 Tab pitáne apne sebakon̲ ko kahá, ki achchhese achahhe bas-
tra láo, aur isko pahináo; aur uske haṭh men̲ angúṭhí, aur
páon̲ men̲ jútí pahináo.
23 Aur wuh motá bachhr̲á idhar láo, aur máro; ki ham kháwen̲
aur ánand karen̲:
24 Kyonki merá yih putra margayá thá, aur pher jitá hai; wuh
kho gayá thá, aur mil gayá hai; tab we ánand karne lage.

HINDUSTA'NI'.

PARABLE OF THE PRODIGAL SON.

In Persian character.

Luke xv. 11—24.

۱۱ ایک شخص کے دو بیٹے تھے * اُن میں سے
۱۲ چھٹکے نے باپ سے کہا کہ ای باپ مال سے جو میرا

حصّہ ہو مجھے دیجے تب اُسنے بقدر معاش اُنھیں
بانٹ دیا *
۱۳ اور بہت روز نہ گذرے تھے کہ چھوٹکے بیٹے نے سب کچھہ
جمع کرکے ایک ملک بعید کا سفر کیا وہاں بدمعاشی میں
اپنا مال برباد کر دیا *
۱۴ اور جب وہ سب کچھہ خرچ کر چکا اُس سرزمین میں
سخت کال پڑا اور وہ بے مایہ ہو چلا *
۱۵ تب وہ جاکے اُس ملک کے ایک متوطن کا نوکر بنا
اُسنے اُسے اپنے کھیتوں پر بھیجا کہ سور چرایا کرے *
۱۶ اور اُسے آرزو تھی کہ اُن چھلکوں سے جو سور کھاتے تھے
اپنا پیٹ بھرے سو بھی کسی نے اُسے نہ دئے *
۱۷ اور جب وہ اپنے ہوش میں آیا تو کہا کہ میرے باپ کے
کتنے ہی مزدورے ہیں جنھیں روٹیاں وافر ہیں اور میں
بھوکھ سے مرتا ہوں *
۱۸ میں اُٹھکر اپنے باپ پاس جاؤنگا اور اُسے کہونگا کہ
اے باپ میں آسمان کا اور تیرا گنہگار ہوں *

١٩ اور اب اس لایق نہیں کہ تیرا بیٹا کہلاؤں مجھے اپنے
مزدوروں میں سے ایک کے مانند بنائے *
٢٠ تب وہ اٹھکر اپنے باپ آیا اور وہ ہنوز دور تھا
کہ اسکے باپ نے اسے دیکھا اور رحم کیا اور دوڑ کے
اسکے گردن پر جا لپٹا اور اسکی مچھلیاں لیں *
٢١ بیٹے نے اسے کہا کہ ای باپ میں نے آسمان کا اور
تیرا گناہ کیا ہی اس لایق نہیں کہ تیرا بیٹا کہلاؤں *
٢٢ تب باپ نے اپنے نوکروں کو کہا اچھی سے
اچھی پوشاک لاؤ اور اسے ملبس کرو اور اسکے ہاتھ میں
انگوٹھی اور پاؤں میں جوتی پہناؤ *
٢٣ اور وہ پالا ہوا بچھڑا لا کے ذبح کرو کہ ہم کھاویں اور انند کریں *
٢٤ کیونکہ میرا یہہ بیٹا مرگیا تھا اب زندہ ہوا کھویا گیا تھا سو ملا
تب وے عیش کرنے لگے *

The above, in Roman character.

11 Ek shakhs ke do beṭe the ;
12 Un-meṇ-se chhuṭke ne bápse kahá, kih ái báp, málse jó merá ḥíṣṣah ho, mujhe dijie ; tab usne baqadari maásh unhen̲ bán̲ṭ diyá.
13 Aur bahut roẓ nah guzre the, kih chhuṭke beṭene sab kuchh

jamạ karke, ek mulk bạídka safar kiyá, wahán bad maạshímen
apná mál barbád kar diyá.
14 Aur jab wuh sab kuchh kharch kar chuká, us sar-zamín men
sakht kál pará, aur wuh bemáyah ho chalá.
15 Tab wuh jáke us mulk ke ek mutawattin ká naukar baná;
usne use apne kheton pur bhejá kih súr charáyá kare
16 Aur use árzu thí kih un chhilkon se jo súr kháte the apná peṭ
bhare; so bhí kisíne use nah diye.
17 Aur jab wuh apne hoshmen áyá to kahá, kih mere báp ke
kitne hí mazúre haín jinhen roṭíán wáfir hain, aur main
bhúkhse martá hún.
18 Main uṭhkar apne báp pás jáúngá, aur use kahúngá, Kih ái
báp, main ásmánká aur terá gunah-gár hún.
19 Aur ab is láyiq nahín kih terá beṭá kahláún; mujhe apne
mazúron men se ek ke mánind banáye.
20 Tab wuh uṭhkar apne báp pás áyá. Aur wuh hanoz dúr thá,
kih uske bapne use dekhá aur raḥm kiyá, aur ḍaurke uske
gardan par já liptá, aur uskí machhiyán lín.
21 Betene use kahá, Kih ái báp, main ne ásmánká aur terá
gunah kiyá hai, is láyiq nahin kih terá beṭá kahláún.
22 Tab bápne apne naukaronko kahá, achchhí se achchhí poshák
lau, aur ise mulabbas karo, aur uske háthmen angúṭhí, aur
páon men jútí pahnau.
23 Aur wuh pálá húá bachhhṛá láke, zabaḥ karo kih ham khá-
wen aur ánand karen;
24 Kyúnkih merá yih beṭá mar gayá thạ, ab zindah húá; khoyá
gayá thá, so milá: Tab we ạish karne lage.

Answers to Objections.

Having thus illustrated the *particular mode* in which the Roman Alphabet may be substituted in place of the principal alphabets in Gangetic India, it seems desirable, though not necessary, to take a brief review of objections that have been advanced against the general substitutionary scheme. *Not necessary*, because many of them have been already anticipated and answered, and to the answer no reply has yet appeared, and no *new* ones have been adduced of a nature sufficiently momentous to counterbalance even *one* of the manifold advantages previously detailed. But *desirable*, inasmuch as total silence may be misconstrued by some into total incompetency to meet the objector on his own chosen field.

The only objections which have appeared in a tangible form, so far as we know, are those brought forward by a correspondent of the Gyananneshun. And as the author has written in a style eminently characterized by freedom from controversial virulence, or offensive personality, he is justly entitled to the most candid hearing. His remarks, therefore, shall be noticed *seriatim*, together with a few others. And in the thoughtful Editor of the Gyananneshun, himself, we doubt not, will be found a most powerful ally.

1. It is alleged, that "the whole native population of India will disapprove of the measure."

This, in fact, seems to be the *gravamen* of all those charges to which our opponents usually appeal. But to what does it amount? To a baseless assumption. No: says the objector, it is not a baseless assumption. But how can this *second* baseless assertion support the *first* baseless assertion? We may assert, that sugar is bitter; that fire is cold; that the sun is black; but what is the use of assertion without proof?* Has the objector proposed to

---

* We can hardly suppose that the objector seriously meant for proof what he states respecting the fabulous origin of the Indian characters. "They," (the Hindus,) says he, "will think, nay feel it sacrilegious to abandon their native characters, which they suppose to have been invented by God," &c. Now, it is *not true* that the Indian characters *generally* are believed to be "invented by God." The *only* character, in regard to which this superstitious belief prevails, is the Deva Nágarí. And that the Hindus have not thought it "sacrilegious" to depart from a form supposed to be communicated by the gods, is *demonstrated* beyond all possibility of doubt, by the *notorious fact, that the natives of every province have actually de-*

offer the shadow of a proof? Not he: a bare, naked, unsubstantiated assertion is all that he favours us with. But this the author must be aware cannot satisfy an ingenuous mind. We feel impelled to push the matter, and ask, *Where* is the proof of so sweeping an assertion to be found? From what *data* can any living creature, with the insignia of truth before his eyes, make a declaration that is *universal*,—without limit, and without qualification? How, where, or when, have "the whole population of India" expressed such decided disapprobation? In what mode have their suffrages been obtained? What meetings, public or private, have been held to discuss this national question? What journals, or pamphlets, have been made the organs of announcing the unanimous verdict? But really thus to press for proof of that which admits of none may seem like forcing a man to make bricks without straw. Suppose we allow, that there *may be* this universal hostility, we must still be permitted to ask, How, or by what means, has it been ascertained actually to exist? Is not the *utmost* that can be said with any semblance of truth simply this,—that *several* natives have manifested dissatisfaction at the measure? And how *can* this amount to a proof, that *all* the natives of Hindustán have done, or will do so? We may *assert*, that the whole of the interior of the Andes is composed of pure gold.

---

parted from that form—have actually invented, substituted, and employed a new and widely different form of their own:—hence the Bengáli, the Uriya character, &c. &c. Besides, have not multitudes of Hindus actually adopted the Persian character to express Indian words, i. e. a foreign character—the character of their hated Mussulman conquerors? Farther still, though the Sanskṛit is believed to be the language, even as the Deva Nágarí is thought to be the character of the gods, strange to say, the natives generally will not read the divine language, if written or printed in the divine character. They prefer writing and reading the Sanskṛit in the common character that is employed in the province to which they belong. Thus, in Bengal, the natives will nót, unless constrained, even learn the Deva Nágarí; neither will they purchase Sanskṛit works printed in that character. They write Sanskṛit in the Bengálí character; and Sanskṛit works printed in it are eagerly sought after, and obtain a speedy, and extensive circulation. After hearing all this, who can any more give heed to the absurd and foolish fable, respecting "the sacrilegiousness" of departing from the alphabetic character of the gods?

When asked for proof, we may reply, In *some* mines gold has been discovered. Indeed, retorts our opponent, Suppose *I* admit that your *universal* assertion *may be* true, how does its truth appear from the *limited* evidence adduced ? *Because* gold has been found to exist in *some* mines, *therefore*, it exists to the extent of composing the *whole* of the interior of this vast mountain range ! If *such* reasoning prove any thing at all, it is this, that sound reason has nothing to do with it.

But we not only deny the *absence* of all evidence ; we negative the assertion altogether. In regard to 999 out of a 1000, is there a *single* circumstance of a *positive* nature, beyond vague analogy and conjecture, to shew that they are either favourable or unfavourable ;—if not ; then, as to the *remaining fraction*, if it be said that some oppose our scheme, we assert, without fear of contradiction, from our own individual experience, *that some do not oppose it, yea, that many highly approve of it.*

After all, supposing what it is utterly impossible to grant, yet, for argument's sake, supposing that it was proved that "the whole population of India" were opposed to the change, what inference should we draw?—That *because* there is "a national prejudice" against it, *therefore*, it should not be attempted ! He who would argue thus, must surely have mistaken the age in which he lives. He must have been dreaming of the times when interested men lazily fattened on ignorance and prejudice, and dreaded all change, as they would the hurricane or the pestilence. And if this master-piece of selfish reasoning, by which the struggle has been maintained to preserve the accumulated prejudices, corruptions, and abuses of ages, and have them consolidated into one imperishable mass of deformity, is to be still echoed and re-echoed in our hearing, the only reply which we can deign to make is, that we are drawing towards the middle of the 19th century, and that such time-serving arguments are fit only to be tossed, like the ravings of the Sibylline oracle, to the four winds of heaven. The grand question with us is :—may the change be pronounced a good one —one, exuberant with blessings to the deluded people of India ?

If so, regardless of abuse, and fearless of difficulty, let us arouse our inmost energies to enforce it on the attention of all around us, and so labour to banish venerated follies, and extinguish for ever "national prejudices."

2. It is said, that as the system "can be adopted (only) on a limited scale at first," those who learn the Roman characters must acquire a knowledge of the native alphabets too, in order to communicate with their countrymen; hence, it is added, "much time will be lost for nothing."

Admitting these premises, we must flatly deny the conclusion. Much time will *not* be lost for nothing. Almost all those who *at first* learn the new system are the boys and young men already engaged, or about to engage, in the study of the English language; and most palpable it is that these must learn the Roman alphabet at any rate; so that to them there can be *no additional* loss of time. Now those who study English will be daily increasing in number and respectability; and these assuredly are the individuals who will give the *tone* to Hindu society. And through their influence and example, hundreds and thousands will gradually become acquainted with the Roman character, who have not studied, nor intend to study the English language; and the necessity for communicating in the native character will be proportionately diminishing. In this way, a knowledge of the system will necessarily overspread every corner of the land, till the number that has mastered the new character, will equal that which has not, and ultimately become preponderant:—then will the necessity for acquiring the native character wholly vanish.

But let us freely and frankly admit that those who live, during the *transition process,* must labour under disadvantages from which their descendants will be exempt: yea, more; let us suppose the disadvantages to be vastly greater than they ever can be:—and what of all this? *Because,* the securing of certain lasting benefits, must be attended with temporary disadvantages, shall we *therefore* sit down in ignoble repose, and make no attempt to secure them at all? To compare *great* things with *small,* what should *we* have been now, had *our* forefathers acted in this despicable *spirit?* What perils by land and by water, what ceaseless anxieties, what painful watchings by night and by day, what cruel persecutions, did they not endure? And for whom did they endure them? Chiefly for us. Boldly did they encounter a thousand difficulties and dangers, which, when overcome, ensured to us the charter of numberless inestimable privileges. And is not the circumstance, that they submitted to such sacrifices, in order to bequeath so rich and noble a legacy to their children, part of their chiefest glory? Is it not this that encircles their brows with the halo of an earthly immortality? Now, in a cause far inferior, it may be, and encompassed with far fewer difficulties, may we not be permitted to emulate so splendid an example? Though destined, we fear, to follow these at an immeasurable distance, still we should not hesitate thus to address the *present* generation of Hindus:—A change has been proposed, which promises to secure for you, and especially those that follow after you, unspeakable benefits. But like every other ameliorating change, it cannot be effected without subjecting you to certain temporary inconveniences. One monitor has arisen who suggests, and by inference, seems to exhort you, not to adventure on the change, because of the great personal trouble with which it may be attended; will you listen to the suggestion—will you brook the exhortation? Long have the Hindus been charged with selfishness and cowardice: will you still perpetuate the grounds of this charge? Rather, will you not arise, and demonstrate to your accusers that you can acquit yourselves like men? Will you not arise and disclaim the imputed baseness of not adopting what is beneficial, merely because it may occasion some additional trouble? Will you not arise, and prove that you are capable of forming disinterested resolutions, and achieving generous deeds—deeds of unfading renown? If the great change now proposed cost *you* some trouble, and subject *you* to the ordeal of opposition and contumely, will it not confer blessings that cannot be numbered, on millions of your countrymen, down to latest posterity?

And in viewing this magnificent prospect, is there not to you a large and ample reward? Is not the very thought enough to inspire your bosoms with the fire of patriotism, stronger and purer far than the glow of heroic chivalry? And as future ages reap the golden fruits of your labour, will they not look back with exulting joy to the present æra; and will not your memories be enshrined, not in "tablets of marble or of brass," but in the far more enduring tablets of the hearts of a grateful and enlightened people?

3. It is asked, "What guarantee have we for the permanency of the system to be introduced? It may happen that a few years hence, an individual holding an entire sway over the Education Committee will dislike the measure, and re-establish the native characters."

Much more importance is here attached to the Public Instruction Committee than it possesses or deserves. Its influence at best can only extend a certain length. But let that pass. Times are now changed. Formerly the Committee acted on the vilest close borough system. Its proceedings were about as well known as those of the court of the king of Timbuctoo in Central Africa. *Hence* the silence and *apparent* acquiescence of the Indian public. But once exposed to view, these proceedings have called forth a cry of indignation throughout the land. And if the veriest despot that ever tyrannized over it with his iron sceptre were once more to attempt to usurp supreme authority, he would be hurled from his throne by the shout of public opinion. If the projected plan succeed *now*, i. e. if a sufficient number of Europeans resolve to support it, backed by the most influential part of the press; if it be, on rational grounds, embraced by numbers of intelligent natives; if it take firm root in some of the most popular seminaries in the country,—we have every possible guarantee, of which such a case can admit, that its demolition is beyond the reach of any future Committee, public or private. In the event of general success, no Committee would dare to interpose its veto; or, if it did, its efforts would prove abortive, and its appeals would be drowned amid the expostulations of an incensed community.

If the measure should be approved of by the present enlightened Committee, and its approbation confirmed by a Government pledge not to sanction any future radical innovation or subversion of it; all good and well. But we repeat it, that the cause is independent of such approbation or pledges. For, if it be as beneficial to India as we believe it to be, it will ultimately succeed by the inherent, irresistible force of those advantages which it so liberally offers.

4. It is supposed to be impossible to establish "one fixed and uniform mode of representing the Indian alphabets in the Roman characters;" because, "there are now several systems, and some stick to this, and some to that, and so on."

This, we verily believe, to be a most groundless assertion. It involves a most dishonourable insinuation. It is built on the hypothesis that numbers of upright men will prefer their own little peculiarities to the securing of national benefits. It supposes, therefore, a compound of pride, selfishness, and infallibility, to the possession of which few, we trust, would have the ambition to aspire. It is, in fact, a libel on the good sense and fair character of many who are not less distinguished as oriental scholars, than as the best friends of the species. The authors of four different systems have been named, viz. Sir William Jones, Dr. Gilchrist, Dr. Carey, and Mr. Yates. The first of these has long since paid the debt of nature; the second is in Europe, far removed from the arena of contest; the third, through the gradual decay of nature, is fast hastening to the close of a glorious career of benevolence; and the fourth, with the genuine feelings of a philanthropist, has voluntarily and cheerfully signified his purpose of abandoning any thing peculiar in his own system, for the sake of the public good, and the establishment of the necessary fixedness and uniformity. A fixed and uniform scheme has, accordingly, been propounded, and it is with no ordinary satisfaction that we refer to the fact, that all who are favourable to the substitution have announced their determination to adhere to it;—and those who are not favourable are not likely soon to trouble us with conflicting representations of the Indian in Roman characters. *That, therefore, which has been pronounced impossible, has already been accomplished.*

But, continues our indefatigable objector, "supposing a new system to be established by common consent, a few years after, some learned persons may find fault with it and make several alterations in it. In this manner, innumerable difficulties will be thrown in the way of the learner."

There is nothing *perfect* under the sun: and if in the time to come, some slight alterations should be proposed and adopted by common consent, such alterations can no more interfere with the general system, or embarrass the minds of the learner, than the substitution of *i* for *e* in *inquirer*, or of *o* for *ou* in *labor*, &c. can be said to throw "innumerable difficulties in the way of the learner" of English orthography.

5. It is urged, that "in case of the substitution of the Roman characters, there must be two sorts of letters, one for printing and the other for writing, and that this is a great inconvenience."

If this be an "inconvenience" in a certain sense, it is one that repays itself with compound interest. What is the perfection of a *printed* character? Is it not a vivid obtrusive *legibility*;—such a legibility that an experienced eye could devour, as it were, at a *single glance*, the contents of a *whole page?* In this respect, the Roman character, as exhibited in the most improved modern type, is unimitated and inimitable.

And no doubt much of this *perfect legibility* arises from the use of *capitals*. This topic has been thus noticed by the intelligent Editor of the Enquirer: "We are still thinking of the new scheme to represent the native sounds by the Roman alphabet. One very great advantage will be gained from the capital and small letters with which the latter abounds. The reading of Sanskṛit, Bengálí, Persian, &c. would not receive an inconsiderable facility if all proper names were to begin with capital initials. This would contribute to render the reading of the native languages much easier than it at present is; and of course this circumstance is, in proportion to the advantage, favourable to the new plan." This is a sound practical observation. Let the reader open the first oriental work that comes in this way, and he will perceive its appositeness. From the first page to the last it will be found to exhibit one continued sheet of homogeneous uniformity. Without being over-fanciful we may compare its internal aspect to that of the plains of Bengal. Here are no undulations of soil—no elevations—no "crags, knolls, or mounds," to diversify the scene, to serve as boundaries to the lords of the soil, or protrude as landmarks to aid the traveller in acquiring a topographical knowledge of the country. Go where you may, it is one wearisome unvaried sameness—one interminable interchange of flat paddy fields and close dingy jungle. Similar is the appearance of an oriental work. It looks like one dull monotonous mass, without beginning, middle, or end. There is nothing *prominent* to point out the commencement of new sentences or paragraphs—nothing *prominent* to distinguish the proper names of persons, places, objects, or events. Wearied and unaided, the reader travels onward. And if he wish to refer to some particular passage, or the account of some particular person, place, &c. he is left in his search without a clew. In a work printed in Roman characters, he would, by the aid of the capitals, *at a single glance* discover what he wanted: in a work printed in oriental characters, he must patiently waste his precious time in plodding through almost every line of every page. Indeed, so great is the inconvenience, that it has been sorely *felt;* and various have been the attempts, by means of *asterisks*, &c. to apply a remedy. But, as yet, every attempt has only turned out a ludicrous failure. Have we not then a right to demand of our mighty Philologists, what expedient *their* imagination, expanded as it must be by its familiarity with the boundless flights of oriental fancy, can now suggest, which may offer a *tithe* of the advantages conferred by Roman capitals?

Still farther, by the beautifully simple device of "Italics," an emphatic word or phrase is made to strike the eye, and thereby reach the understanding or the heart, with an ease and rapidity that almost surpasses conception, and sets description at defiance. In this particular, we should like to know what imaginable contrivance equally *simple* and *perfect* could be devised for any one of the Indian alphabets? and yet, in reading, how can the importance of such an admirable contrivance be too much exaggerated?*

Again, what is the *perfection* of a *written* character? It is not *facility of formation*, combined with *distinctness?* In this respect the Roman character is unimitated and inimitable. The form of the *written* letters is not so different from that of the *printed*, as to demand much additional time in mastering it,—and that little time is *more* than compensated for by the almost incredible *speed* with which it can be employed in practice.

There are, besides, other *peculiar* advantages. Men may contrive to disguise the fact as they may, nevertheless, it is not the less certain, that, though *nominally* or *theoretically*, the *printed* and *written* oriental character is the *same; practically*, there is a difference as wide, and often wider, than between the printed and written Roman character. The truth is, that that form which an-

* That no one may think this over-stated, let the following quotation from Murray's large grammar be duly weighed: "On the right management of the emphasis depends the life of pronunciation. If no emphasis be placed on any words, not only will discourse be rendered heavy and lifeless, but the meaning often left ambiguous. If the emphasis be placed wrong, we shall prevent and confound the meaning wholly. To give a common instance, such a simple question as this, "Do you ride to town to-day?" is capable of no fewer than four different acceptations, according as the emphasis is differently placed on the words. If it be pronounced thus: "Do *you* ride to town to-day," the answer may naturally be, "No, we send a servant in our stead." If thus: "Do you *ride* to town to day?" Answer, "No, we intend to walk." "Do you ride *to town* to day?" "No, we ride into the country." "Do you ride to town *to-day?*" "No, but we shall go to-morrow." Now if so much of the meaning and force, and often so much of the beauty and propriety of an expression, depends on the emphatic word, is it not of the highest importance that it should be distinctly marked? From the example now given may not the most obtuse understanding perceive, with what matchless ease, simplicity, and effect, this can be done, by means of italic letters?—And may we not challenge all the orientalists in the world to concoct, if they can, an expedient which, with the *same* ease, simplicity, and effect, can single out an emphatic term or expression in any of the Indian languages, if written or printed in the Indian characters?

swers best in print is far too stiff, angular, or rounded, to suit the *speed* that is so very *desirable* in *writing*. Hence it happens that a Hindu or Mussulman, when he writes his own alphabetic character, with any degree of quickness, almost invariably finds himself constrained to depart from the precision and regularity of the printed form, yea, to depart so far from it, that his writing is often illegible to all but himself, and not unfrequently even to himself. More than this: as there is no acknowledged standard of written character, one man departs from the printed standard in one way, and another, in another. Hence, necessarily arises a grotesque medley of characters, a "rudis indigestaque moles" of varying forms. Each man, in fact, may have his own system of written character, and there may be as many systems as there are writers. How inextricable then must be the resulting confusion?

Compared with this unavoidable chaos, how orderly and complete is the Anglo-Roman system. Here all is regularity and harmony. There is one universally acknowledged standard of written, as well as of printed, character,—even that which unites in the highest possible degree, quickness in forming, and distinctness when formed. And this standard being established by common consent, the deviations of particular individuals therefrom, being only variations more or less minute from what is fixed and uniform, they never do, they never can lose their similitude or identity with the original. One man can never fail to understand his own writing: and all men must be able to decypher the writing of all men. So far, therefore, from the *distinct written form* being an "inconvenience," in practice; it must be hailed as one of the greatest and happiest "conveniences," which the wit of man ever suggested, or his ingenuity contrived.

6. It is assured, that "all the useful books that have been and will be published in the native characters before such a change takes place must be reprinted in the Roman;" and then follows the wondering exclamation, "What an immense expense will be incurred in the reprinting of such works as Babu Rámcomal Sen's English and Bengálí Dictionary, Dr. Carey's quarto Dictionary of the Bengálí and English," &c.

Surely there is an utter fallacy or oversight in this objection. How stands the case? Is the printing of *one* edition of a book like the opening of a perennial spring, which, when it once begins to flow, will continue to pour forth its exhaustless waters *for ever?* If it is, we grant, that the printing of another edition in the same or in a different character may be said to incur an *extra* expense, large or small, according to the size of the work. But it is not so: one edition, consisting as it does of a limited number of copies, is obviously exhaustible; and when all the copies are sold, it is of course exhausted. What then must be done? What else can be done, but to print a *new* edition, in order to meet the growing wants of a rising community?—and if a *new* edition of a good book *must* be called for, in the natural order of events, *may* it not be printed in one alphabetic character, as well as another, without incurring an "immense" additional expense, or any additional expense at all? *May* not even the expense of such a reprint be vastly less than that of the original edition?

But it is added, that the Indian letters, in consequence of the inherent vowel and particular combinations, may be compressed into as small a space as the Roman. It is needless to argue this point abstractly. It resolves itself into a simple matter of fact; and the best answer that can be given is, to advise the reader to look back, and, inspecting the specimens supplied in this article, let the testimony of the visual organs decide the question in debate.

7. It is objected, that by the proposed substitution, we deprive the present generation of the means of mental and moral improvement.

This is founded on a total misconception of our design. It is not in our power, nor if it were, would we ever propose to suppress all the existing publications, and supply no more in the same form. We know that there are hundreds and thousands of adults acquainted with the native character, who can never be expected to learn any other. And *suddenly* to deprive them of works which they can peruse, and the perusal of which is calculated to elevate and purify their minds, were either a species of inquisitorial cruelty or a sort of wicked madness. Enthusiastic and visionary as we are reputed to be, we have not yet suspended the functions of sober reason. Our object is, by all lawful means, to disseminate the knowledge of a system which we verily believe to be fraught with blessings innumerable to this benighted land. With this view, books in every department of religion, literature, and science will be immediately prepared and published on the improved plan. The mode of reading these with intelligence, will be taught to those over whom our influence extends; and every reasonable encouragement will be held out to all who desire to propagate the knowledge of it. By these means the superiority of the reformed system will be *gradually* perceived, and its advantages duly appreciated; till at length it may be divulged to the extent of absorbing all the prevailing systems. In other words, the native alphabets retiring before the Roman, and being naturally displaced by its incumbent and increasing weight, will eventually, without violence or alarm, disappear from off the land.

But during the *intermediate process*, books will be supplied to the adherents of the old systems, that are to sink fast into decrepitude and final annihilation. That is, for a season, there will be two contiguous and contemporaneous streams—the old and the new—the former decreasing, and the latter increasing, in volume—the one contracting itself within narrower bounds, and the other enlarging its borders; till at last *both* channels become *one*, on whose broad and expanded bosom shall flow the fresh waters that are to scatter fertility and abundance over a dry and parched land. Or, to drop the metaphor, we shall, for some time to come, have to furnish two sets of books—the one in the native, and the other in the Roman character. With the former we shall supply chiefly the aged; with the latter, chiefly the young, especially those who learn English. Let then the School Book Society, the Bible Society, the Tract Society, &c. provide themselves with books of the two kinds now mentioned, wherewith to supply these two classes of readers. And as the *new* order of things gains ground, the copies in Roman character will abound more and more, till they gradually supersede those printed in the native form. And, when great numbers of the reading population come to understand and prefer the new arrangement, then may the Sumachar Durpun, and other journals especially designed for natives, exchange their Indian for the Roman garb. And then may we witness the sublime spectacle of all books, pamphlets, magazines, and journals unitedly pouring forth floods of knowledge, through one consistent and harmonious medium, over every region of the largest and fairest empire under the sun!*

---

* That cavillers may no longer taunt us with the sneering question :—"Having now settled your alphabetic scheme, what use are ye going to make of it?" it may be stated, that we have *already begun* to apply it to its legitimate purpose. The following works are *now* in preparation, and some of them *already passing through the press*; viz.

1. The New Testament, English and Bengálí. The Bengálí version, in Roman character: to be published in single Gospels.

2. The New Testament, English and Hindustání. Do. Do.

3. Woollaston's Grammar, Bengálí and Hindustání.

4. Moral Precepts, English and Hindustání verse.

5. Scientific Dialogues, &c. &c.

6. The Elementary English works, or Primers, prepared for the General Assembly's Institution, Calcutta, viz.

No. I. Instructor, interlinear Bengálí version, in Bengálí character, to be afterwards followed by the Roman.

No. II. Do. literal version in Bengálí character, and free version in Roman.

No. III. Do. entirely in Roman character.

We trust it will now be seen that we are in right earnest, and that our scheme is not to evaporate in mere words. And as our earnest desire is to give offence to none, but do good to all, we sincerely hope that many, who are now lukewarm, or even decidedly opposed to us, may yet be conciliated and become our staunchest friends and supporters.

Since we wish, with the least possible delay, to translate Primers, Grammars, Histories, &c. into every language and dialect in the presidency of Bengal, we would respectfully solicit the assistance of such European and Native gentlemen as are competent to the task of translation. If any one who is qualified will kindly undertake to translate one or more works into the language or dialect with which he is acquainted, he will be immediately supplied with a copy, on application. When completed, the work will be printed free of expense to him, and he will be furnished *gratis* with a large number of copies for distribution. Already have some gentlemen promptly volunteered their valuable services; and others, who

The foregoing are all the objections which we have seen advanced; and whether in themselves, and especially in contradistinction to the manifold advantages pointed out in a former paper, they can be allowed to possess "the weight of a feather," we leave to the candid reader to judge. Some, as fully anticipated, have again sounded the tocsin of "the letters, the letters, what is the learning of letters? A trifle, a trifle, a mere trifle." Reasons which have *not* yet been controverted were formerly given for dissenting *in toto* from the burden of this song. And if farther confirmation be required, it may now be furnished. Some years ago, when controversy ran high respecting the merits of Dr. Gilchrist's philological labours, these found an advocate in the Edinburgh Review. The Quarterly, on the other hand, with its tremulous dread of all change, treated the learned orientalist with lofty disdain. But in spite of the most deadly hostility, the current of change has set in, and who can now arrest its progress? Even the Quarterly, which still doggedly clings to many antiquated errors, has in some things changed. On the present question even it has let in some gleams of light. In the last No. or the No. for October, there is an able Review of Grimm's New German Grammar. In his elaborate introduction, this author, in the genuine German style, has a lengthy dissertation on the origin and descent of the ancient European languages,—the Gothic, the German, the Saxon, the Celtic, the Sclavonic, &c. Now mark the Reviewer's words:—

---

cannot lend their aid in translation, have decisively expressed their good will, by forwarding liberal donations to defray part of the expense that must, in the first instance, be necessarily incurred.

Besides providing translations of useful works, and printing these in Roman character, it is our intention, if supported by an enlightened public, to select every oriental book that is worth any thing, and turn it into the new orthography, *i. e.* Romanize it. In this way we may expect that the good, or at least the harmless, will help to swell the accumulating body of sound literature—while the bad and worthless will be abandoned to neglect, and left to perish as they deserve.

The entire series of Native works and translations, we may designate "*The Romanized Series of Oriental Literature.*"

"The first 600 pages of the book are taken up with a minute examination of the letters in each of the dialects which come under consideration, *and here we must commend the example Grimm has shewn in abolishing the use of the Gothic characters.* There is no more reason for our employing them, than for our using the Roman capitals in printing Latin; the common type was equally unknown to both nations, and the use of the uncouth Gothic letters, both increases the difficulty to the reader, and adds to the expense of printing, without affording any countervailing advantage. *Indeed, the example might be extended even to the oriental languages with very great benefit; if, for instance, the Sanscrit were printed in European characters, we are convinced that a large class of persons would acquire at least its rudiments, who are now deterred from similar studies by the formidable difficulty of a new character looking them in the face at the very outset.*"

With such a respectable authority as this on our side, we can afford to allow objectors to regale themselves undisturbed with the music of their own favourite fancies.

Having now developed our plans, our *expository* task is ended. Henceforward "action" shall be our watchword. We have a field before us wider and nobler far than any which aroused the ambition of the Eternal City in the meridian of her glory:—but, oh, how vastly different our object in entering it! Where *she* would have marched at the head of conquering legions, satisfied when terror established the invincibility of her arms—*we* go forth with the messengers of peace, the heralds of true wisdom, satisfied only when happiness, harmony, and love shall proclaim the invincible kindness of Truth. And those treasures of knowledge which surpass a thousandfold what Rome in her proudest days ever possessed, we shall disperse through the medium of *forms* which her inventive genius has supplied. And thus, along distant streams and fertile valleys, never visited by the Imperial Eagle, shall the name of "Roman" flourish in connection with the mental emancipation of millions, when all other stately monuments, that recal the remembrance of Roman greatness, shall have crumbled into dust.

ALPHA.

P. S. It has been already stated, that during the last month, several friendly communications have been received respecting the substitution of the Roman in place of the Indian alphabets, and our "scheme" for accomplishing that end. Amongst these is one from a gentleman in the Upper Provinces, well acquainted with the Oriental languages, and successfully engaged in the instruction of Native youth—on which accounts we deem his remarks particularly entitled to attention. Besides this, his letter briefly alludes to certain advantages attending the proposed substitution that wholly escaped our notice; we have, therefore, much satisfaction in making from it the following weighty extract. After various introductory remarks the author thus proceeds :—

"I entirely agree with you, not because the idea is yours, but because the measure is fraught with incalculable advantages to India. It is, I really and truly believe, the most effectual mode of *any*, of diffusing knowledge, *both* Asiatic and European, among the people at large. The grand barrier to improvement in this country has been the want of *printing*, or the being obliged to impart knowledge through the slow, limited, difficult process of manuscripts. It is a most expensive and Herculean labour to *print* in the Arabic, or Persian, or Deva Nágarí character. It would be quite as easy as printing any English work, to print books and newspapers, &c. in Roman characters, though the language be different. The benefits of *printing* their *own* books in this way would be a thousandfold—but the benefits of printing in the Urdu dialect, and Roman characters, the substance of our literature, are quite incalculable. Nothing could impart a greater impulse to civilization. Every gentleman almost might then publish translations—for there are but few indeed who cannot explain in *Urdu*, their thoughts, or the substance of any written work. Epistolary correspondence between Europeans and

Natives (now next to impossible, owing to the necessity of employing a third person as the medium of communication), would become as common as correspondence is between two Europeans, or two Natives, in their respective tongues. A judge might then read all the proceedings *himself*, and write his orders *himself*. Public functionaries would then perform, singly and unaided, twice the work, which they now cannot perform without the assistance of three or four Natives. It would lead to the adoption of thousands of European *words*, in the Urdu books and compositions, and thus the Native literature would be enriched most rapidly :—but there is no end to the advantages I anticipate from this most ingenious plan," &c. &c.

TO THE PEOPLE OF HINDUSTAN.

All who read newspapers, those winged messengers of intelligence, now know that a proposal has lately been made to write Sanskṛit, Persian, Bangálí, and other Indian languages in the letters of the English alphabet. But many do not exactly understand the *nature* and *object* of the proposal. These, therefore, it is proper briefly to explain, and let the wise and intelligent among the natives of India lend an attentive ear.

First. The *nature* of the proposal is simply this.—That in writing and printing words, sentences, or books, in Sanskṛit, Persian, Bangálí, &c. English characters should be used for *all*, instead of Deva-Nágarí, Persian, or Bangálí characters. Thus instead of writing the word किसी in Nágarí characters, we might write kisí in English characters : instead of باپسے in Persian, bápse in English characters : instead of পিতাকে in Bangálí, pitáke in English characters : and so, in like manner, might we write *all* other words in *every* Indian language in English characters. In this way, *one* alphabet, i. e. *the English*, might answer the purpose of *all the Indian alphabets*.

Now, why should this proposal appear *strange* to the natives of India? Have not they themselves long been accustomed to write the words of one language in letters belonging to another? Is not this fact known to all except Harís, Majurs, Dhángars, &c., who are so miserably ignorant, that they know nothing? For example: has not the Persian character been often practically used in representing Indian words, particularly in the Upper and Western Provinces? And on the other hand, has not the Nágarí character been employed in expressing Persian and Arabic terms? The Urdu, which is a compound of Persian and Indian words, has been represented indifferently by Persian or Nágarí letters. And if so, why not this, and other Indian languages, by the English? Besides, do not Bráhman Pundits, the Kúlin editor of the Chundrika, the Mahá Rájá Kálíkrishan Báhádur, and all other learned and respectable natives, write Sanskrit words and slokes in Bangálí characters? And if so, why might they not write Sanskṛit slokes in English characters? the characters of the language of the rulers of this land—a language, which is dignified also by possessing boundless treasures of knowledge to make men good and wise, great and powerful?

To shew how easily this might be done, we here present one or two specimens:—

SANSKṚIT SLOKES.

In Deva-Nágarí Characters.

अनेक संशयोच्छेदि परोक्षार्थस्य दर्शकं ।
सर्व्वस्य लोचनं शास्त्रं यस्य नास्त्यन्ध एव सः ॥

In Bangálí.

অনেক সংশয়োচ্ছেদি পরোক্ষার্থস্য দর্শকং ।
সর্ব্বস্য লোচনং শাস্ত্রং যস্য নাস্ত্যন্ধ এব সঃ ॥

In Roman.

Aneka sanshay ochchhedi parokshárthasya darshakang
Sarvasya lochanang shástrang yasya nástyandha eva sah.

Meaning.

He who is not possessed of learning, which dispels many doubts, points out hidden things, and is the organ of sight to all, is even as a blind man.

STANZA.

Arabic.

اِصْنَعْ بِنَا مَا اَنْتَ لَهُ اَهْلُهُ
وَلَا تَفْعَلْ بِنَا مَا نَحْنُ لَهُ اَهْلُهُ

Persian.

اصنع بنا ما انت له اهله
و لا تفعل بنا ما نحن له اهله

Iṣnạ bíná má anta lahu ahluhu,
Wa lá tafạl bíná má naḥnu lahu ahluhu.

Meaning.

Do to us what is worthy of thyself; but do not to us what we deserve.

Second. The *object* of the proposal may be briefly stated to be *the benefit of the people.*

Some through ignorance, and others from sinister motives, have declared, that the object is to perplex and injure the natives by destroying their vernacular languages. Now the opposite of this is the *true* statement. *One grand object is to benefit the people by preserving, enriching, and facilitating the study of, the native languages.* Instead of perplexing people's minds, the proposal of substituting *one* in place of a *multiplicity* of different alphabets, is the only sure way of delivering them out of all perplexity.

If a Hindu* has several *khejur*† trees in his garden, and if his neighbour proposes to cut them down and plant a *ním*‡ tree in their place:—this proposal must be injurious. But if his neighbour proposes to cut down the *khejur* trees, and plant a very large *mango* tree, which will every year be covered with the finest fruit, in their place:—would this proposal be injurious? No, all will unanimously reply, it would not be attended with injury, but real benefit. Precisely similar is the case in regard to the present proposal. It is not intended to supplant the native alphabets by the introduction of another of inferior value, for that would not be good: but it is proposed to supplant these alphabets by the introduction of one that shall secure *numberless advantages,* which all the rest combined, do *not* possess:—and must not this be pronounced good? Surely it must. And in order that no one may any longer impose upon you in this matter, some of the benefits of the proposal will now be stated. We speak to the wise and intelligent among the Hindus. Let the wise and intelligent judge.

1. In most of the Indian alphabets, there are about fifty letters, with innumerable compounds, which greatly perplex and retard learners. Now all these can be perfectly represented by 24 simple English letters, with the occasional use of these three simple marks, (′) (.) (-) This it is plain, must make the progress of every learner more easy and rapid.

2. All who wish to be useful in business, renowned for learning, or exalted to high situations and responsible offices, must learn the English language. If then, all learn to read and write the Eng-

---

* Wherever Hindu occurs in these remarks, it denotes a native of Hindustán, whether Hindus or Mussalmáns.

† A tree that produces an inferior sort of fruit.

‡ A tree whose fruit cannot be eaten.

lish alphabet from the time of infancy, when learning their own mother tongue, much valuable time and much useless trouble must be saved in acquiring a knowledge of the English language.

3. Besides learning English, great numbers of Hindus are obliged to learn several Indian languages. But it is well known that much valuable time is consumed by the majority of mankind in learning the *new* characters of any language. And a vast deal of time is spent in acquiring the *same facility* and *speed* in reading and writing these characters, as is enjoyed in reading and writing those with which they are long familiar. Now whole months or even whole years of unprofitable labour may be saved by the universal introduction of the English characters.

4. The Sanskṛit is the common root of all the Indian dialects. But at present each dialect has letters of a different figure; and this leads the Hindus of one province to suppose that the Hindus of another province speak a totally different language. Consequently, they are apt to regard each other as strangers and foreigners. Now, if all the Indian dialects were presented in the *same English character*, it would be *seen* and *felt* that the natives are not divided into so many sections of foreigners to each other, that they have *all fundamentally* the *same* language, and that without much difficulty, a community of interest, and a beneficial reciprocation of thought might be effected to an extent at present unknown, and from the repulsive aspect of so many written characters, deemed utterly impracticable.

5. It follows from this statement, that as almost all Indian dialects are derived from the Sanskṛit, when a native thoroughly masters one dialect, he is already acquainted with the meaning of numberless words in every other. If all were, therefore, represented in the same English character, instead of learning one, or two, or three languages, as at present, a Pandit, Shástrí, or Munshí, might in the course of his lifetime master *all* the languages of Hindustán. Surely, that proposal which would lead to the accumulation of so much learning in the mind of one person must be super-excellent.

6. By the admirable contrivance of Capital and Italic letters in the English alphabet, the facility of reading with propriety, and referring to names and particular passages, is mightily increased. But from the nature and shape of the Indian letters, this contrivance cannot be imitated. If then English letters be substituted in their place, the thousands, and the tens of thousands of Hindu youth may have the unspeakable benefit of this simple and beautiful contrivance in learning to read and write their own vernacular languages. Stops in all their several gradations, marks of interrogation and admiration, inverted commas, and other aids to the correct reading and understanding of books and manuscripts which the native literature at present either does not possess at all, or possesses in a very imperfec tdegree, will be at the same time introduced; and this, it must be acknowledged, will save time, increase knowledge, and lead to the native languages becoming fixed and cultivated much sooner than it would be possible for them to become without such helps.

7. It is a fact that, from the intricacy, the complexity of most of the Indian characters, it is utterly impossible to reduce them to so small a size as the Roman may be, without rendering them altogether indistinct, or even illegible. In this way, twice the quantity of paper, and nearly twice the quantity of binding materials and labour must be lavished for nought. In other words, books printed in the Indian characters will cost *nearly double* what the same books would cost if printed in the English characters. And must not Hindu parents rejoice at the success of a plan that promises to save *half* the amount which they would otherwise have to pay for books in the education of their children? And must not the proposal that would save *so many rupees* to *every Hindu parent annually* be one of the *best* ever announced in this land?

8. As the multiplicity of different characters creates numberless difficulties in the way of studying the native languages, the mines of learning which those are said to possess, remain unexplored from age to age. Consequently, the treasures of knowledge

contained in them, continue hidden and concealed not only from Europeans, but from natives themselves. No native, not even a Bhaṭṭáchárjya, though so learned as to deserve the epithet of Mahá-mahopádhyá, can ever expect to know a tenth part of the lucubrations of his ancestors, so long as there is such a variety of written characters. And if even a Hindu Pandit cannot know a tenth part of the strange and rare histories, philologies, rhetorics, logics, metaphysics, astronomies, geographies, and theologies, which have been accumulated by the sages of Hindustán—will not unlearned natives and the Pandits of other countries begin to suspect that there are no such stores in existence? How then can such suspicions be removed? How can it be shewn to all people, in every land, that the Hindus possess such wonderful piles of written shasters, which at present lie concealed from view, behind thick jungles of new and strangely varied characters? What plan can be imagined half so well adapted to this purpose, as that now proposed, viz. to transcribe the whole of their writings, if the Hindus so wish it, into *one* uniform character, that is *already universally known*—known by all the civilized and learned in Europe, Asia, Africa, and America?

If they were to do this, the Hindus would only be following the example of the English themselves. Formerly the English language was written in various peculiar characters, which were known by the names of Saxon, German text, &c. but by degrees all these were discarded, and the Roman character (which is the one at present used in writing English) was adopted in place of them all. Now do you suppose that the existing English literature was obscured by this change? On the contrary, as the language now became transferred into a character which was universally current throughout the civilized world, the general knowledge of it was greatly promoted; and to this day, when it is desired to bring into notice books or manuscripts in any of the old characters, they are as a matter of course turned into the Roman characters, and they then become at once accessible to the whole world. If, therefore, any body should hereafter object to the plan of changing the character, let this be your answer, *that the most civilized and prosperous nation in the world have already tried it, and that the experiment has been attended with complete success.* What ground of confidence as to what is good can we have so sure as the experience of the wise?

Instead, therefore, of obscuring the Hindu literature, and tarnishing the merits of Hindu authors, as some ignorantly suppose, this plan is the best possible for bringing the whole range of Hindu literature to light, and loading the Hindu authors with such honours as they deserve. The change of characters produces no change in words, dates, or names. All the words of the Indian languages, all historical dates, and all proper names of persons, places, and events, remain unchanged, and so far as this plan is concerned, unchangeable. If then, the Hindus really wish that they should no longer be accounted ignorant or barbarous—if they really wish that all nations on earth should know what prodigious masses of singular writings they possess—they ought immediately to combine in one grand association, and resolve to write, print, and publish all their books in English characters. If they do this, the whole civilized world may know the extent of their merits.

That no one may presume to doubt the truth of this representation, we refer to the No. of the Quarterly Review published in London, in the month of October, last year. This work, as many of the learned Hindus already know, is one of the highest literary authorities, not only in Europe, but in the whole world. Now hear, what the Quarterly Review says:—"If the Sanskṛit were printed in European (meaning Roman or English) characters, we are convinced that a large class of persons would acquire at least its rudiments, who are now deterred from similar studies by the formidable appearance of a new character looking them in the face at the very outset." Here then is a glorious field of ambition open to the wise and learned among the Hindus. If they transcribe all their works in English characters, their literature, science, and religion will be known throughout Europe, and every country of the civilized world.

Who then is so blind, as not to discern the marvellous excellencies of the plan now proposed ?

The foregoing are *some* of the manifold advantages which would attend the substitution of the English in place of the Indian alphabets. They may be thus briefly summed up :—

1. The substitution of the English alphabet would facilitate the progress of a Hindu in learning his own vernacular language.

2. It would facilitate his progress in learning the English language.

3. It would facilitate his progress in learning several other languages, necessary to the carrying on of business.

4. It would break down the barriers that at present separate the Hindus from one another, and lead to free communication, and a beneficial interchange of sentiment throughout the land.

5. It would enable Hindus of ordinary ability and perseverance to master almost all the languages of India, and so put it in their power to benefit its countless tribes and families.

6. It would greatly assist young and old in reading, writing, &c., any language, with precision and propriety.

7. It would save a great deal of money, to every Hindu parent, by greatly diminishing the price of books.

8. It would bring to light the entire mass of Hindu literature, science, and theology, and make the claims of Hindu authors known to all the learned in the four quarters of the world.

More advantages might easily be enumerated : but are not those amply sufficient to prove the excellency of the present proposal ? Are not these more than sufficient to demonstrate, that it is fraught with the richest blessings to the people of Hindustán ? And if so, however unintentionally, are not those the enemies of the people who object to and oppose it ? And are not those the best friends of the people, who are its most strenuous advocates ?

We speak unto you as unto wise; judge ye.

A TRUE FRIEND TO THE NATIVES.

ON THE ADAPTATION OF THE ROMAN ALPHABET TO THE ORTHOGRAPHY OF ORIENTAL LANGUAGES.

(Extracted from the JOURNAL OF THE ASIATIC SOCIETY *for June,* 1834.*)*

All who have devoted themselves to the acquirement of any of the languages of India must have experienced in the irreconcileable difference of the alphabets of the East and West a stumbling block in the porch of their studies, and a source of constant doubt and difficulty, whenever the occasion has arisen for expressing in the letters of their mother tongue sounds and vocables belonging to any of those languages. It is the scholar's object to write the words so that they shall be read with a correct pronunciation by the uninitiated, and at the same time show the true spelling of the original. He seeks therefore the letters of known pronunciation that come nearest, not only to the sounds he desires to represent, but likewise to the letters used in the language from which the word is taken. Unfortunately it is not always easy to find letters that will answer this double purpose, and the difficulty is much increased by the circumstance, that all the vowels and several of the consonants in use have more than one sound in the same language of Europe, and some of them half a dozen sounds at least, if the varieties of all the countries which use the Roman alphabet are taken into account. What then was to be done when India fell into European hands, and the necessity arose for continually writing Indian words in books and public correspondence? Every one at first of course had to decide for himself, and unfortunately they who commenced the work of writing Asiatic names in the alphabets of Europe were not scholars. At present we shall confine ourselves to the proceedings of our own countrymen in this respect, putting out of view all reference to the modes of writing adopted in France and Germany, and elsewhere, and those in particular which have been adopted recently, in consequence of the efforts making by the literati of Europe, to bring into vogue the

Sanscrit language and its literature, at the very time that the half informed of our countrymen are seeking to discredit both here.

It would appear that they who first had occasion to write in English the names or words of the East, bethought themselves of the sounds in that language which came nearest to those they desired to represent, and spelled the words accordingly: thus *sipahee* was very generally spelt *seapoy*, doubtless from the similarity of its sound to the well known word *teapoy*, and in the jargon of the day, *Surajood-doula* was corrupted into *Sir Roger Dowler*, and *Allahabad* become known as the *Isle of Bats.* Many absurdities of this description might be pointed out were it our object to seek them: even Governor HOLWELL, though himself a Bengalee scholar, has in his printed tracts, *Morattors—Shaw Zadda—Genana—Patsha—Shaw Allum—Phirmaund—Metre* (for *Mitur*), &c. &c. He has also *Sou Raja Dowla* which is nearly as ridiculous as the English knighthood of that Nuwab.

This method of writing from the ear did very well so long as it was the half-informed addressing the absolutely ignorant. The transmutations were precisely of the same description as those of which we find examples, not only in the Greek and Roman methods of writing Teutonic and Asiatic names, but in the Leghorn and Cales of the old English writers of the past century, the Naples and Venice of the present day, and the Ecosse and Galles and Espagne, into which the less pronounceable native names of those countries have been softened in France.

But as the knowledge of the languages of the East extended, and they who had to write became themselves well acquainted with the true pronunciation and orthography of the words and names they were using, and felt likewise that they were addressing others as well informed upon the subject as themselves, they began to seek the means of spelling true—that is, of using in English corresponding letters for those used in the language from which the word or name might be taken. The Persian and Arabic are languages that have long been known in Europe, and the force and power of each of the letters of those alphabets have accordingly been attempted to be expressed in various ways, according to the native country of the interpreter; but the first we believe who accurately gave to the public the Nagree, Devanagree, and Bengalee alphabets was Mr. HALHED in the Preface to his version of the Code of Hindoo Law, compiled under the orders of WARREN HASTINGS in 1775. His consonants correspond very nearly with those of Sir WILLIAM JONES's alphabet, except that he makes no distinction between the hard and soft *d, t, dh,* and *th.* The short vowel अ he writes with a short *ĕ*, the letter इ with a double *ĕe,* bearing similarly the short mark: ऐ, is expressed by *ăe;* ऐ, he writes *ī* and औ, *ŏu.* Every vowel according to this system had its long or short mark above it, which was very inconvenient either for printing or writing.

When the Asiatic Society was established, Sir WILLIAM JONES saw the necessity of introducing a consistent mode of writing all Indian words. Not satisfied with this system of Mr. HALHED, he devised the alphabet that bears his name, and is still used by that learned body in its proceedings; but neither the influence nor the reputation of this great linguist was sufficient to procure for his alphabet the general adoption so desirable, and indeed so essential, to the purpose he had in view. It continued as a sort of Devanagree for the learned *par excellence;* a style of writing to be reverenced and respected, but not imitated. In spite of every endeavour to recommend the Society's alphabet for universal use, the business of the country continued to be conducted either in the jargon spelling first adopted from similarity of sound, or with the *ad libitum* improvements of those, who, knowing the correct spelling of the original, adopted the letters they thought best calculated to express the true sound of the words properly pronounced. It is now near fifty years since the attempt was first made to introduce this obvious benefit of a consistent and correct alphabet, and yet Sir WILLIAM JONES's mode of writing has gained no ground in India, whatever may have been its fate elsewhere. What can have been the reason for this? Does not the fact itself afford irrefragable evidence that there must be some inherent defect in the system that induced its rejection, and led to others being preferred. There it was, recommended by the Asiatic Society, composed of the principal civil servants, and of all in the military, clerical, and medical professions, who were entitled by knowledge of the subject, or by situation, to take the lead in such a matter. There was this Society, periodically putting forth its volumes, and all its principal members publishing their works according to the orthography of the illustrious founder; yet no one out of the pale, and not all of those within it, could be brought to spell names, in their correspondence, as the Society spelt them. For fifty years this tree of Sir WILLIAM JONES'S planting has been stationary or has grown like the aloe repulsive and disagreeable, living still, but putting forth no branches and yielding no fruit. Who after this can say that there must not be something in this system repugnant to the ideas and preconceived notions of those whose language is English? The powers and pronunciations given to the different letters are manifestly not such as have been recognized and adopted as just and appropriate by those who read and write that language. Another system has gained ground in its stead, and to its prejudice, and this in spite of the great names of JONES and COLEBROOKE and WILSON, whose adherence to the antiquated style has prevented its sinking into absolute disuse and oblivion. Let us inquire then what is this other system, and what the claims it possesses to the preference of the unlearned.

Towards the close of Lord CORNWALLIS'S government, Dr. JOHN BORTHWICK GILCHRIST produced his Dictionary and Grammar of the Hindoostanee language, and as matter of necessity, prefaced both by explaining the force of all the letters in use in the language, and the corresponding vowels and consonants of the Roman alphabet, by which he proposed to express them. The difference between his system and that of Sir WILLIAM JONES lies entirely in the vowels: the short unexpressed letter अ which Mr. HALHED wrote *ĕ* was written *a* by Sir WILLIAM JONES and *u* by Dr. GILCHRIST; the *ĕe* and *ēe* of HALHED, *i*, *ì* of Sir W. JONES, were rendered *i* and *ee* by GILCHRIST; the *ŏo, ōo*, of HALHED, *u, ū* of JONES, were expressed by *oo ;* and the *ī, ai*, of the two former systems by *y*, corrected but not improved to *ue ;* and lastly, the *ŏu* of HALHED and *au* of JONES by *ou* corrected to *uo*.

The more taking and popular part of this system lies evidently in the use of the short *u* instead of *a*, for the silent unexpressed inherent letter of the languages of India : people could not be brought to write *bat* for the sound of *but, tab* for *tub*, and *patee* for *putee*. Having the choice therefore, they discarded the letter which never in any of the words of any of the languages within their knowledge had the sound it was proposed to give to it. The adoption of *oo*, instead of Sir W. JONES's *u*, followed as a necessary consequence of the appropriation of *u* to the short sound ; and *au* for the sound of *ow* in how was so unnatural, that it was gladly discarded for *ou*.

It does not appear that the Government took any part, until very recently, in promoting the use of one or other of these systems : they had each therefore a fair field and no favor for thirty years at least. During the whole of that period the knowledge of the languages was extending, and the old jargon was disappearing from all the public departments, finding only a sanctuary and stronghold that bade defiance to all reform within the precincts of the Supreme Court. The issue was in a decided leaning from the first to the system of GILCHRIST. This has now been that of all official correspondence for fifteen or twenty years at least, whereas it will not be found that the orthography of Sir WILLIAM JONES has taken root in any single department, pertinaciously as certain learned individuals of high authority have adhered to it.

In 1822, the design was conceived of forming an accurate record in the English language and character of all the land tenures of the country. It was felt to be necessary to determine upon some alphabet or system, for the conversion of names correctly, prior to the formation of these registers, and then first did the Government officers indicate any system under authority for preference. The merits of each method were fully weighed and consi-

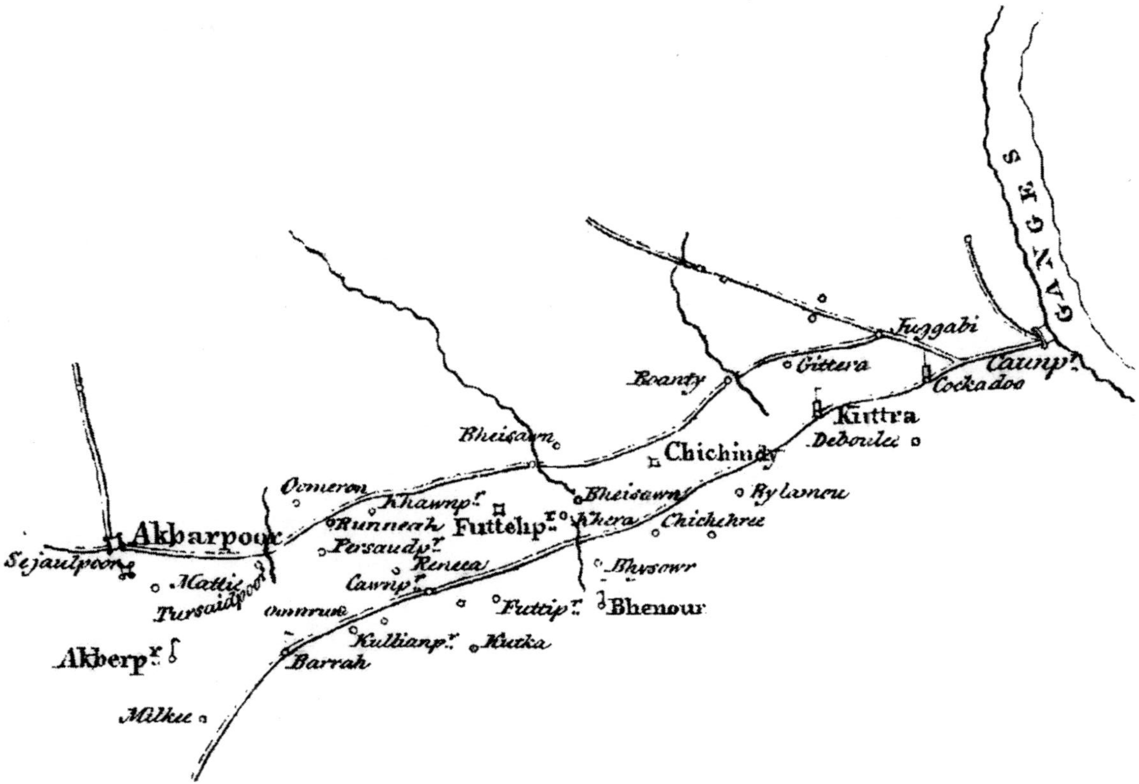
GANGES
Caunp.r
Cockadoo
Juggabi
Gittera
Kuttra
Deboulee
Roanty
Chichindy
Bheisawn
Rylamou
Bheisawn
Khera
Chichehree
Bhusowr
Bhenour
Futtelp.r
Khawnp.r
Runneah
Persaudp.r
Reneea
Cawnp.r
Futtip.r
Kutka
Kulliamp.r
Barrah
Oomeron
Omnrue
Akbarpour
Sejaulpoor
Mattie
Tursaidpoor
Akberp.r
Milkue

dered, prior to the determination, and the scheme of GILCHRIST was adopted, simplified by the rejection of some of his quaint methods of expressing the nicer distinctions of sound. This alphabet was circulated, and great progress was made all over the country in producing registers, in which the names of persons, and places, and properties were so written that no one could hereafter find difficulty in writing them back, into any given character, upon bare inspection.

Contemporaneously with this measure, and as part of the same scheme, revenue surveys were put in hand, and maps on a large scale were constructed, in which the names of every place or object were accurately entered according to the same system. Up to this time, no attempt had ever been made to make this grand improvement in the geography of India. The maps of Bengal were copied to the letter from the surveys of RENNELL made in the era of jargon, and though better spelt than most of the documents of that period, yet still partaking largely of the miscellaneous mode of writing, so liable to mislead. All the surveyors subsequently employed had been left to pick up the names of places by the ear, and it had never been made an instruction to them to ascertain how they were written in any dialect or language of India, and to transfer them according to system into their maps. The surveyors too unfortunately were very seldom scholars. In order to show the consequences of this neglect, and to expose at once the absurdity of trusting to the ear in a matter of this kind, an extract is annexed* from a map of the Dooab, compiled not ten years ago, and now in our possession: it bears the official signature of the surveyor-general of the day, and professes to be from the best materials then in the archives of that department. In this extract it will be seen that the well known road from Cawnpoor (Kanhpoor) to Ukburpoor is laid down double, being taken apparently from two routes made with compasses, or theodolites, varying in a small degree, so as to give a different direction, and the

* See Plate.

copyists of the surveyor-general's department have not discovered that the routes are the same, *because all the names are spelled differently*. There are regularly

Kuttra,	Gittera,
Chichehree,	Chichindy,
Bhysour,	Bhysawn, Bheisawn, (Bhenour ?)
Fattip^{r}.	Futtehp^{r}.
Reneea,	Runneah,
Oomrun,	Oomeron.

With sundry other names, till one road comes to Akberpoor and the other to Akbarpoor, the relative distances of all these places being the same. Like absurdities might be shown in many maps similarly constructed from materials, in which the names have been set down by the ear without the observance of any system of spelling. It is no fault of the map compiler if he has not recognized Chicheree to be the same place as Chichindy, and Kuttra as Gittera, when they stand in two maps in positions not exactly corresponding. The fault was in the employment of an officer to survey, without instructing him specifically how he was to write the names of his map. The revenue surveys, so far as they went, effectually corrected this error; and what is more, the maps, constructed by the officers employed in this department, are capable of being converted with confidence into any character, without each name being as at present, an object of separate inquiry and research, whenever it is desired to publish a map in the Persian, the Hindee, or in any other character of the country.

But to return to our subject: the Record Committees, wheresoever they were established, succeeded entirely in reforming the orthography of names in the zila dufturs. That they did not do more, but after involving considerable expence, failed to provide the desired land registers, was owing to many causes, which need not be discussed here. The effect of these institutions in confirming the use of the Gilchristian system is all we have now to do with: that effect will we presume not be denied. The leaning had been to this system for thirty years before, but at last the act of Government, and the specific exertions of all public officers throughout the country, continued for nearly eight years consecutively while the Committees lasted, fixed and established this system of Gilchrist, as the orthography of office and of business. Even though there were not in it any innate inherent superiority or grounds for preference, even were it the inferior system of the two, still this fact ought, one would think, to secure it from any hasty attempt at change. Except there be some obvious apparent defects pointed out, the undoubted ascertainment of which has been the result of actual experience, would it not be madness to think of discarding what had been so established? What then is to be thought of this new attempt of Mr. TREVELYAN, to set up again the rejected alphabet of Sir WILLIAM JONES, and by the gratuitous circulation of thousands of copies to diffuse and disseminate, as if from authority, a system fully and formally tried and found wanting?

The Journal of the Asiatic Society, being a work of science, conducted under the special countenance and support of that Society, will always be respected for the matter it contains; and it signifies little in what garb it may choose to present its Asiatic names. Allowance will be made for the consistency of the Society's adherence to the system of its venerable founder, and all that read its proceedings know well what they have to expect, and are prepared to encounter familiar letters applied to strange uses after the manner practised by this Society for half a century. But now that the Gilchristian method of writing has been so long established for record, for surveys, and for making familiar to the uninitiated public, the sounds and names of Hindoostan, every official man and every man of sense must protest against the present attempt to introduce once more the discarded system, one too that from its use of the *a* for the short *u* would change the spelling of every word and name from one end of India to the other.

Let the Sir WILLIAM JONES's system, his *a* and his *i*, *í*, and his long and short *u* be reserved, like the Devanagree, for recondite science: there his alphabet has its footing, and no one desires to eject it from its stronghold: but for business let us have our current Nagree, the short *u* and the *ee*, and the *oo*, which have grown into use from their ready adaptation to the ear, and from the preference secured for them by all the associations of sound to letters, which we have been accustomed to from our infancy.

In the pages of the Journal there has appeared a notice laudatory of Mr. TREVELYAN's attempt to effect by a *coup de main* a change in all the established methods of writing mofussil names. As this Journal has now for itself so wide a circulation in the interior, it is necessary that its pages should not be made to serve the party views of the advocates of any one exclusive system, but that the merits of each in its particular line should be fairly stated. The Sanscrit scholar will perhaps find his advantage in following the alphabet of Sir WILLIAM JONES, which is that of the grammars and dictionaries, and of most of the translations from that language; but he that is content with the Persic, Oordoo, or the familiar literature of Hindoostan, the man of business and of the world, will find all the books, the dictionaries, and grammars, and vocabularies, to which he is in the habit of referring, and all the records and public documents that fall under his observation, written uniformly in the character of GILCHRIST. There is little fear that even the weight of the Journal's recommendation will be successful in superseding what is so established. If the world were not wide enough to hold both systems—if the order had gone forth from CÆSAR, that one only should stand, and the issue were, a *bellum ad internecionem* between the two—then might the Journal fitly advocate the cause of its scientific mode of writing to save it from destruction and the sponge: but so long as there is no attempt to encroach on the ground it occupies, or to interfere with its peculiar province in literature; while it is suffered to luxuriate in the paradise of Sanscrit, without any attempt to foist in its rival, even as an humble companion of its pleasures in that Eden of joy; why should the votaries of this learned system strive to gain for it an universal dominion, for which it has been found unfitted, and assume the offensive against the system in use for business? Let each retain its own, and both abide together in peace and good will and harmony, holding forth in the facilities they jointly offer an invitation to all people to adopt either one or the other, accordingly as they find either most convenient for their purpose, and under the assurance that the object, which is to obtain such a method of writing as shall afford a ready means of transferring the word back into its native character, will equally be accomplished, whichever may be the character adopted. Both systems represent perfectly to the scholar the letters used in the original languages, but it is contended that the GILCHRIST alphabet, as now generally introduced and used in the public offices of this presidency, conveys to the uninitiated a more correct and true notion of the proper pronunciation, than the antiquated and rejected system of Sir WILLIAM JONES, and therefore is the best adapted to business. Through the pages of the Journal let the European public of India be undeceived on this point. The attempt to dislodge the system of GILCHRIST is entirely a matter of individual speculation, and is certainly not the result of any inconvenience felt, or dissatisfaction expressed with it, by the Government, or by any class of public officers or persons whatsoever.

H. T. P.

DEFENCE OF SIR WILLIAM JONES' SYSTEM.

It seems now to be admitted with scarcely a dissenting voice that the plan of expressing the languages of the East in the English character offers the best and nearest prospect of fixing and enriching the Native Dialects, and of establishing a common medium of communication, epistolary as well as oral, between the people and their rulers—that great desideratum, the absence of which has always so much impeded the due administration of justice in this country, and stood in the way of our taking root in the affections of our subjects to the extent, which the rectitude of our acts and intentions might entitle us to expect. The principle, therefore, that the languages of the East should be expressed in the character of the West, and that by degrees one written character should be made to pervade the whole world, has been admitted by a decided majority of those persons who from their education and habits of mind are qualified to give an opinion on the subject. The only question which remains to be discussed is the particular orthography, or in other words, the particular mode of applying the European characters to the Asiatic languages which it is most desirable to adopt. Hitherto public opinion has been divided between two systems, one of which (the Italian system), from its having been first introduced into the East by Sir W. Jones, is generally known by that distinguished scholar's name, and the other system was invented by Mr. Gilchrist and is called after his name.

It is necessary to premise, that, as far as the consonants are concerned, there is no discrepancy between the two systems worth contending about. The only difference between them is in the vowels and diphthongs, and even in this case only in some of them, while in others both systems exactly agree: but in order that the reader may have the subject clearly before him, we will subjoin a table of the vowels and diphthongs of both systems.

Sir William Jones'.

a-*a*bove	á-*a*rt
i-*i*n	í-Police
u-P*u*sh	ú-r*u*le
e-there	ai-*a*isle
o-Note	au-C*au*sa [Latin pronunciation]

Dr. Gilchrist's.

u-Cull*	a-Call
i-Kill	ee-Keel*
oo-wool*	oo-Cool*
e-there	ue-chyle*
o-Cole	uo-Cowl*

* The letters marked thus * are expressed differently in the two systems.

Out of ten vowels and diphthong sounds, therefore, four are expressed alike in both systems, which reduces the field of contest between the two systems to within very narrow limits. Taking consonants and vowels together, there are about seventy different variations of sounds in Hindusthani, of which only six are expressed differently. This is the utmost extent of the quarrel between the shade of Sir Wm. Jones and Dr. Gilchrist.

We shall endeavour to state as briefly as possible the relative advantages and disadvantages of the two systems.

Sir Wm. Jones' Plan is systematic and complete in all its parts, so that in every case in which an analogy exists between different sounds, a corresponding analogy will be found to pervade the signs by which they are represented. Thus the long sound of *a* is *á*, of *i*, *í*; and of *u*, *ú*; and the diphthong *ai*, which is compounded of *a* and *i*, is represented by those letters, and *au* (*ow*) which is compounded of *a* and *u*, by *au*. The consequence of this strict attention to preserve an analogy in the sign corresponding to the variations in the sound is, that the acquisition of the Alphabet is greatly facilitated to the learner, who in fact has to make himself acquainted with only five elementary signs which are the representatives of as many original sounds, and the remaining five are only elongated forms or composites of these.—He has to learn *a*, *i*, *u*, *e*, *o*, and *á* is only the long form of *a* distinguished by the usual mark, *í* of *i*, and *ú* of *u*, and *ai* is the composite of *a* and *i*, and *au* of *a* and *u*.

In Dr. Gilchrist's plan, with a single exception, there is no analogy whatever between the long and short forms of the vowels, and between the diphthongs and their component vowels. Thus in his system *a* is the long form of *u*, *ee* of *i*, and the diphthong *ai* is represented by *ue*, and *au* by *uo*. It is needless to dilate on the confusion which this want of system must produce in the mind of every learner. No help is here provided for him, and instead of being guided from step to step by a change in the form of the character, sufficient to distinguish the modification in the sound, while enough is retained of the original letter to mark the elementary connection, he is perplexed by a variety of characters between which no kind of analogy is capable of being traced. In short, instead of having only five signs to get by heart, he has no less than nine. In tracing the analogy between corresponding modifications of sound, this plan is worse than if no assistance were afforded him. In this eccentric system of letters long vowels are actually divorced from their partners and so disguised as to render it impossible to recognize the original connection between them, and diphthongs are in like manner kidnapped from their parent vowels, and disfigured worse than gypsey children. Who would suppose that *u* is the legitimate husband of *a*, that *ee* is the devoted wife of *i*, that *ue* is the interesting offspring of *a* and *i*, and *uo* the eldest hope of *a* and *u*. This is not a system of *orthography;* but, if I may be allowed to invent a word, of *kakography;* of confusion, mystification and absurdity. It is singular that when a man sat down with a carte blanche before him to invent a system of letters, he was not able to devise something better than this; and it is still more so that having the labours of his learned predecessor Sir W. Jones to profit by when he altered, he should have altered so much for the worse.

Another advantage of Sir W. Jones's plan is that, besides being complete in itself, owing tot he perfect analogy which exists between the different letters, it bears a strict correspondence throughout to the great Indian or Deva Nagari alphabet. All the alphabets derived from the latter are very systematic, and a scheme which is otherwise cannot properly represent them. But Sir W. Jones does it exactly as will be seen from the following table:

अ *a*	आ *á*
इ *i*	ई *í*
उ *u*	ऊ *ú*
ए *e*	ऐ *ai*
ओ *o*	औ *au*

The natives of India are therefore already quite familiar with the idea of distinguishing the modification of sound by a corresponding modification of sign, and when they see the same plan adopted in the anglified version of the alphabet, they immediately recognize the propriety of it, and enter into the spirit of the scheme. As the new orthography is mainly intended for the people of India, the circumstance of its being entirely coincident with their preconceived feelings and ideas must be allowed to be an advantage of no small importance.

It is hardly necessary to observe, that no kind of analogy exists between Dr. Gilchrist's and the Indian or Deva Nagari alphabet. When an Indian reads Sir William Jones's alphabet, he sees a long *á* immediately succeeding the short *a*; a long *í* the short *i*, and a long *ú* the short *u* (the long vowel being in each case distinguished by a mark as in the Sanscrit) which is just what his previous knowledge would lead him to expect, but when he comes to Dr. Gilchrist's plan, he finds *a* following *u*, and *ee* following *i*. What therefore would be his opinion of the comparative merits of the two systems? Would he not say, that one is in every respect as complete as the alphabet of the Gods (Deva Nágari) while the other is an inexplicable mass of confusion.

Another advantage attending Sir William Jones's system is that it is not only analogous to, but is the very system itself which is used in expressing Latin and all its derivations; that is, Italian, Spanish, French, &c. It is true that in England we do not pronounce Latin in this way, but this is only because we have barbarized it, and made it accord with our Saxon pronunciation. Even in Scotland and Ireland, to say nothing of continental Europe, they read Latin exactly in the way in which it is now proposed to read Hindusthani. This entire coincidence of the new Hindusthani orthography with the orthography of the learned language of the whole of Europe, and with that of most of its colloquial languages, is a point of great importance. Even in the present age its advantage will be felt, in so far as the learned all over Europe, and in most cases the vulgar also, will by this means obtain direct access to our Indian Literature; and what is still more deserving of consideration, a foundation will be laid for the establishment in due time of an uniform system of orthography throughout the world.

This is an object, which, however distant the prospect of accomplishing it may be, no man who has the slightest regard for posterity, should ever lose sight of. Next to the establishment of an universal language, that grand desideratum of the philosopher and the philanthropist, the establishment of an universal system of orthography will most tend to the production of unrestricted freedom of intercourse between all the families of the human race; and the one has also a direct tendency to bring about the other. Now if Gilchrist's plan were to be generally maintained in India, so far from having advanced a step towards this grand result, we should make a decidedly retrograde movement, and the proceeding would be tantamount to shutting the door to the possibility of an uniform system of writing and printing being ever adopted in the eastern and western hemispheres. Gilchrist's plan is utterly abhorrent from the Roman family of languages, and it does not even coincide with the English, as will be shewn hereafter.

Sir William Jones' plan has a simple character for every simple sound, while in Dr. Gilchrist's simple sounds are in three instances expressed by double letters [ee, oo and oo]. This, to say the best of it, is an extremely clumsy contrivance, and in the business of nations and course of ages it would lead to an immense unnecessary expenditure of time and money. That this is the case, may be seen by taking the example of a single sentence,

Bees tees moorghabee huen toomharee peechee,

which in Sir William Jones' orthography would be

Bís tís murghábí hain tumhárí pichí

There are 38 letters in this sentence written according to Dr. Gilchrist's plan, and only 30 if it be written according to Jones; that is to say, in only six words the former exceeds the latter by no less than 8 letters. Apply this to a book, and conceive the waste of types, paper, and valuable time which must result from it. Supposing an octavo volume, printed according to Sir William Jones's plan, to consist of 500 pages, and each page to contain on an average 304 words, the total number of words in the volume would be 1,52,000, and if the same volume were printed according to Mr. Gilchrist's plan, then at the rate of 8 additional letters for every six words, the number of extra letters will amount to 1,90,000, which would make an addition to the book of 136 pages, and instead of consisting of 500 pages it would consist of 636. Apply this to the entire Literature of half the world through a succession of ages, and conceive the result, if you can. If this average is considered to be above the mark, I have no objection to suppose that every six of Gilchrist's words contain only half the number of double letters which those above instanced do, and at this rate the book printed according to Gilchrist's plan would exceed what it would be if printed according to Sir William Jones' plan by 68 pages.

Lastly, there are three characters in Gilchrist's alphabet which do not belong to English or to any other language under the sun which we have ever heard of. These are *ω*, *ue* and *uo*. With the exception of the pupils of Dr. Gilchrist who, from early associations and respect to their master, may naturally be expected to be admirers of his scheme, these characters are utterly barbarous to every description of people; and it is therefore impossible for them to secure a general recognition for themselves in the breasts either of Englishmen, European Foreigners or Indians. Sir William Jones' plan, as has been before stated, contains no arbitrary sounds whatever, but is in every respect in strict accordance with the Latin and Latino-European languages. Even the *au*, of which no example is to be found in English, is perfectly familiar to every Scotchman and Irishman who knows Latin, and if a youth at Dublin College or the High School at Edinburgh were to pronounce *causa* like *cawsa* he would be immediately corrected and told to sound it *cowsa*, and the same of course every where on the continent of Europe.

It will be proper in this place to say a few words in regard to the general principles of the two systems, and the causes which have led to their respective adoption. Sir William Jones well knew, that the Romans and the Indians derive their origin from the same family of the human race, and that the analogy which is every where perceptible in their mythology and their language extends also in a high degree to their alphabets. The arrangement of both is exactly the same. In both the same letters have exactly the same powers, and while one is the most perfect alphabet in the east, the other is acknowledged to bear the palm in the west.

Sir William Jones also knew that, when the barbarous Saxon Monks came to apply this alphabet to their language, they did it without any regard to system, and took no pains to preserve the original powers of the letters. *i* was pushed out of its place by *ee*, and made to do duty for *ai*. *a* was generally superseded by *u*, and the services of *u* having been pre-occupied in this manner, *oo* was made to officiate for it. Even this arrangement was by no means constantly adhered to, and thousands of instances might be mentioned of the application of the same letter to several different sounds and of different letters to the same sound. The English system of spelling in short (I protest against its being called *orthography*) is a labyrinth, a chaos, an absurdity, a disgrace to our age and nation. It forms the principal difficulty of our language (which is the more provoking as there is nothing in the structure of English which calls for it) and causes annually increasing millions in all the four quarters of the globe an enormous unnecessary expenditure of valuable time, and still more valuable temper. The amount of vexation and discouragement and loss of time which is caused every year, particularly to foreigners, by the extremely incorrect way of spelling now in use, is incalculable.

But to return to the subject immediately under consideration, Sir William Jones and Dr. Gilchrist had two systems of letters before them; one of which was acknowledged to be the most perfect which the wit of man had ever devised, and in every respect corresponded with the systems already in use in India and on the continent of Europe; and the other was perhaps the most imperfect the world had ever beheld, and totally differed from those which prevailed both in the East and West, England and North

America alone excepted. Sir William Jones was a noble Philologist. He imitated the universal governor as far as it is permitted to man to do so, and embracing the whole world in his view, married the East and West by promoting by his sanction and influence the adoption in both hemispheres of the same mode of writing. As his object was to fertilize the whole world, he drew from the fountain head; but Gilchrist limited himself to the narrow circle of English spelling, and by the adoption of that corrupt, eccentric system, opposed an effectual bar to his system ever extending beyond his pupils and the readers of his own books.

It should be borne in mind that Sir William Jones and Mr. Gilchrist both drew from the mine of English letters, and that the only difference between them was that one appropriated the dross, while the other culled the pure gold. Gilchrist chose the most corrupt and imperfect parts of our system, while Jones selected those which were consistent with true principles and coincided with the most perfect alphabets both of the East and West. The *í* in *Políce* is almost as well known in English as the double *ee* in *feel*. The *u* in *pull* is certainly better known than oo which is pure Gilchristian. The *ú* in *rule* is as familiar as the double *oo* in *cool*. The *ai* in *aisle* is assuredly far more common than *ue*, which is another arbitrary sign to be found no where except in the books printed by Dr. Gilchrist himself. The *au* in *causa* (Latin pronunciation) is also better understood than *uo*, which is another Gilchristian hieroglyphic; and even the short *a*, the stumbling block of our Gilchristian friends is quite as familiar to us as their favorite *u*, and any body who will take the trouble to look in the English Dictionary, will see it used at the commencement of 500 words like *above*, *about*, *abound*, and so forth.

It has fallen to the lot of our generation to introduce the English letters into India, and the simple question for us to determine was, whether we should choose that part of the English literary system which is corrupt and limited, or that which is complete and universal. Since most Europeans in India are from their youth thoroughly imbued with Gilchrist's system, if we had desired to obtain an ephemeral popularity, we must have chosen the least perfect plan; but this was not our object. We were not concerting plans for the satisfaction of a few hundred Europeans. The benefit of the hundreds of millions of our dark faced brethren of Asia was our aim, and therefore, undeterred by the clamor which we foresaw would be raised by a portion of our countrymen wedded by education and habit to the system we felt ourselves called upon to reject, we adopted the notation which was most perfect in the abstract, and which most nearly corresponded with Indian and European feelings.

It will be satisfactory to our friends to know what we have ourselves but lately become acquainted with, that a few years ago when the American Missionaries first committed the language of the Sandwich Islands to writing, they adopted this same Italian Orthography, the standard of which has now been raised in India. This is a remarkable testimony to the intrinsic excellence of the system. Two bodies of people belonging to different nations, and situated nearly on opposite sides of the Globe, were called upon to deliberate independently of each other, regarding the choice of a system of letters, which it was proposed to introduce into less civilized countries, and what was the result? Their selection both fell upon the Italian system, thus confirming what had previously been maintained regarding its superiority over all the other European systems. Ought not this fact to encourage us to proceed with energy and zeal? The Americans are the natural allies of our nation for the diffusion of every good word and work throughout the world, and we joyfully hail their accession as our colleagues in the establishment of a correct universal system of letters. The following list of Sandwich Island words, expressed both in the old and new style, extracted from a History of the American Mission in those Islands, is annexed.

NAMES OF THE ISLANDS.

Improved Spelling.	*Former Spelling.*
Ha-wai-i.	Hah-wye-e. Owhyhee.
Mau-i.	Mow-ee.

Improved Spelling.	*Former Spelling.*
Mo-lo-kai.	Mo-lo-kye.
O-a-hu.	O-ah-hoo.
Kau-ai.	Kow-eye.

MISSIONARY STATIONS.

Ho-no-lu-lu.	Ho-no-loo-loo.
Wai-me-a.	Wye-may-ah.
La-hai-na.	Lah-hye-nah.
Kai-lu-a.	Kye-lu-ah.
Wai-a-ke-a.	Wye-ah-kay-ah.

NAMES OF PERSONS.

Ke-o-pu-o-la-ni.	Kay-o-poo-o-lah-nee.
Li-ho-Li-ho.	Lee-ho-Lee-ho.
Ka-u-mu-a-li-i.	Kah-oo-moo-ah-lee-ee.
Ho-a-pi-li.	Ho-ah-pee-lee.
Ka-pi-o-la-ni.	Kah-pee-o-lah-nee.
Ku-a-ki-ni.	Koo-ah-kee-nee.
Po-ki.	Po-kee.
Wa-hi-ne-pi-o.	Wah-hee-nay-pee-o.
Pu-a-a-i-ki.	Poo-ah-ah-ee-kee.
Ka-ma-kau.	Kah-mah-kow.
Ka-lai-o-pu.	Kay-lye-o-poo.
Pau-a-hi.	Pow-ah-hee.
Ke-kau-o-no-hi.	Ke-kow-o-no-hee.

It only remains to meet an argument of our adversaries which has been put forth by one of them with an air of anticipated triumph. "Sir William Jones's Plan," they say, "has been well known for these sixty years and yet it has made no sensible progress;" from which they conclude, that it never will make any. To this we reply, that God mocks at the short sighted sagacity of mankind by sometimes bringing to nought their best devised schemes, and at other times he vindicates his own authority and proclaims to the world that the Most High ruleth in the kingdom of men, by bringing about mighty changes by means apparently the most inadequate, and at times the most unexpected. The use of gunpowder was confined to fire-works, and Steam power was treated as a plaything long before these great elements took their proper place in the system of human affairs: but, to pass over minor instances, was not Christianity, the system which is destined to bring back the world to its obedience to the Lord of the universe, and to make it that abode of purity and peace and unalloyed felicity which it was originally intended to be—was not this glorious revelation confined for about 1500 years within the narrow limits of the Holy Land until Christ appeared on earth and commanded his followers to make it known to all mankind?

There is no lack of scourges and blessings in the storehouse of God, and things can be turned by him in his own good time and way to uses of which we can at present form no conception. Is it not conformable with our experience of the rules under which the divine government of the world is carried on, that the Christian Philosopher who consecrated his learning to the glory of his God and the good of his fellow-creatures—that the Christian Scholar who did not hesitate to make the following solemn declaration, which will be recorded to the latest posterity; "I have regularly "and attentively read the Holy Scriptures; and am of opinion, "that this volume, independently of its divine origin, contains "more sublimity and beauty, more pure morality, more important "history, and finer strains of poetry and eloquence, than can be "collected from all other books, in whatever age or language they "may have been composed," that such a man should be blest in the work of his hands, and that the seed sown by him should in God's own time spring forth and cast its shoots far and wide throughout the East? Let who will gainsay it, Sir Wm. Jones has laid a good foundation, and future ages will bless him as the father of the literature of the Eastern Hemisphere. "Cast thy grain before the waters,* and thou shalt see it after many days."

To descend to secondary causes, why has Sir Wm. Jones's system heretofore not made greater progress? Simply because no body ever thought of making it a *popular* system. Where is the Primer, the Spelling Book, the Grammar, or the Vocabulary which was ever published on this plan with a view to popular edu-

* Alluding to the method of sowing in the East.

cation? The utmost which its advocates have hitherto aimed at has been to fix it as the medium of *scientific nomenclature*, and in this they have *fully* succeeded. That it has not gone further is not the fault of the system, but of its admirers, who till lately never once attempted to extend it beyond these limits. As far as it has been tried, it has completely answered every expectation that was entertained of it, which is no small praise, and gives us promise of continued successful results. The system has completely obtained the acquiescence of the learned all over the world, and, if we mistake not, it will in the course of a few generations obtain the assent of the vulgar also.

On the other hand, Why has Gilchrist's system made the progress it has? Simply because he wrote and taught and published. What is his system except his books and lectures? Without these it could have no existence. It is a remarkable fact, that Gilchrist's plan has never made any spontaneous progress, and we never heard of a single school except his own in which it is taught, or of a single book that was ever printed in it except by him. From this it would appear that it has no inherent virtue, no self-operating principle, calculated to secure for it success independent of the exertions of the founder. It will apparently live and die with him. It has met with just that degree of success which might have been expected from the determined perseverance of its author, and from his personal and official influence, and it has not gone a step beyond this. The Doctor himself is its moving principle. Let him relax his efforts, and it is nothing.

But what a different picture does Sir Wm. Jones's system at this moment present? After having completely stood the test of learned criticism—after having gone through a probationary period of sixty years, and approved itself to the great body of scientific men throughout the world, it has been claimed for popular use. The jewel must no longer remain shut up in the casket, but must be brought forth to shine in the face of day. The money must no longer remain hoarded in the treasury. The time has come to spend it for the general advantage. The gold needs no assay. It has been well and thoroughly tried, and all that is required is to put it into circulation.

Three Printing Presses, of which one enjoys a more extensive business than any other in Calcutta, and another is the most influential of the Provincial Presses, are at this moment actively engaged in preparing Picture Alphabets, Primers, Spelling Books, Readers, Dictionaries and Grammars, and two Lithographic Presses are employed in providing writing Copies and Pictorial Illustrations. Daily assurances of support are received from all parts of India. Numerous public officers and almost all the leaders in the education of the country are on our side, and if we make the same progress during the ensuing three months, which we have done for the last three, the system will become so firmly established that nothing less than a violent persecution will be able to uproot it.

C. E. T.

27th August, 1834.

THE END.